ROADRUNNER *or* ROADKILL

*Business Essentials
When Failure Is Not An Option*

David Morrison

Cognoscente Press
Newmarket, Ontario, Canada. 2010

Text Copyright © 2010 Cognoscente Consulting Limited.

Cartoons Copyright © Randy Glasbergen. Reprinted with permission.

Mention of specific companies, products, processes or services does not constitute or imply a recommendation or endorsement by Cognoscente Consulting. All registered or trademarked company; product, process and/or service names mentioned are property of their respective entity. Links mentioned are provided as a reference to assist in identifying and locating other Internet resources that may be of interest. Cognoscente Consulting does not assume responsibility for the accuracy or appropriateness of the information contained in other sites, nor does it endorse the viewpoints expressed in other sites.

All rights reserved. The use of any part if this publication reproduced, transmitted in any form or by any means electronic, mechanical, photocopying, recording, or otherwise, or restored in a retrieval system, without the prior written consent of the publisher is an infringement of the copyright law.

ISBN: 1450503071
ISBN-13: 9781450503075

Edited by Mike Muxlow

Cover design by George Athanasiou

PREFACE

When I began writing this book, we were knee deep in the worst recession of many decades. Corporate downsizing, layoffs, early retirement, and boomers looking for a new career has created an opportunity for the economy to bootstrap itself to the expansion of small and medium businesses.

In the past, it was small business and not larger companies like General Motors that have led every exit in recessions. However, with the soft stock market and high debt ratios, new entrepreneurs cannot tolerate failure. More now than ever, it is simply not an option.

This book is dedicated to new entrepreneurs and is designed to help them avoid the mistakes so commonly made as businesses expand.

"Analysis of business failures made over many years, shows that a high percentage of these failures was due to unqualified or inexperienced management."
Bank of America, "Small Business Reporter".

INTRODUCTION

Whether you control your business by spreadsheets, accounting software or an Enterprise Requirements Planning System, the information in this book is for you. There are many business books that give advice on topics like marketing, finance and management, and each has its place however, few of them focus on the little things that a small and intermediate sized business owner must absolutely get right to survive and prosper.

You probably remember the battles between Warner Brothers®' Roadrunner and Wiley Coyote. The Roadrunner always stuck to his core competitive advantage - speed and agility, and no matter how many schemes Wiley came up with to catch him, the Roadrunner always survived! The take-away from this cartoon - there are many more ways to fail than there are to succeed.

In today's economic environment many people are starting businesses after being downsized, de-hired, laid off or let go. Success is mandatory. Many of the aspects that need to be watched and managed to avoid failure are not the sexy fun things like orders and deals. Simply put, they are the plain old core management issues that include cash flow, processes and systems.

I wrote this book based on some of my past experiences that caused me to contemplate why we so often have to learn from our own mistakes and not from others?

The first epiphany occurred when writing my Master's thesis. I went to the library to look at past works and I found that they all focused on successful but often trivial ideas. We called them the 'Platinum Bridge Projects' as they could never be implemented. I also knew from several colleagues that many of their theories did not prove out experimentally. Then I thought, "Wouldn't it be great if they told someone in a thesis so that the errors were not repeated?"

The second revelation came during my long career with IBM. Many errors were made simply by not performing adequate initial investigation. Fortunately, IBM had deep pockets and could bring a huge amount of very good resources to fix or contain the errors. Most small and intermediate sized businesses do not have this luxury.

Lastly, in running and consulting for start-ups during the technology explosion and collapse of the late 1990's, I discovered that companies continued to make the same mistakes over and over again. In the beginning, people even threw money at businesses for what turned out to be dumb Internet-based ideas. In the end, the money dried up and many of these companies did not have the essentials in place to survive. And at the same time, there are many success stories like Google, Yahoo and others.

So what was the difference?

According to an old proverb, "You learn everything you are going to learn, the first time you get kicked in the head by a mule". This book is the summation of over 30 years experience in making mistakes and boiling them down to the essentials. I deliberately set out to make this a short book that can be easily read by busy people. It covers a lot of subjects but to make the essentials come to the surface, I have only included enough examples for an understanding of the importance of the essentials. I have also supplied references you can check out for further explanation.

"Roadrunner or Roadkill" cannot promise success. Nor can any other business book for that matter. Success comes from a good idea, the right timing, adequate funding, entrepreneurial drive and a lot of luck. What I can promise is that if you follow the business essentials discussed in this book, you will encounter far less pain on your road to success.

So, what are the essentials?
- Start with a good idea and test it
- Get your positioning right
- Get your funding in line
- Manage cash and expenses like they are your own
- Build processes and systems for where you want to be
- Hire and manage your people effectively
- Balance marketing and sales, and measure everything
- Look for the signs of trouble and act quickly
- Never forget your customers!

Visit My Blog: http://roadrunnerorroadkill.typepad.com/

> **WARNING!**
> Ignoring the road signs posted in this book could be hazardous to the health of your business! Those who will get the most out of this book are those who know what they don't know. If you get even one business-saving idea from this book, then it has been a success.

"A wise man learns from the mistakes of others, a fool makes them for himself."

Anonymous

TABLE OF CONTENTS

Chapter 1 – Start with a good idea 1

Chapter 2 – Get your positioning right 15

Chapter 3 – Secure your funding................... 23

Chapter 4 – Cash management 39

Chapter 5 – Process engineering is not 55
            just for big companies

Chapter 6 – Hire and manage people effectively...... 65

Chapter 7 – Balance marketing and sales 73

Chapter 8 – When trouble emerges................. 97

Chapter 9 – Checklist for the future 109

Appendix.. 117

Glossary 131

CHAPTER 1
Start with a good idea

"Man's mind, once stretched by a new idea, never regains its original dimensions"
Oliver Wendell Holmes, Jr.

ROADRUNNER TECHNOLOGIES

Bob Abbot was a middle manager for a large corporation. In the downturn he was given a severance package as well as his vested pension. He had retirement savings and a modest investment portfolio. His kids had left the nest and his wife still worked. He was 52 years old and still wanted to work. He had an idea for a new product and now was the time to take a risk and make it work. He set up the structure of a company and started to plan out what kind of cash and facilities he would need. He was willing to take on the risk of starting a business, but failure could wipe out his savings and put him back into a position of looking for a new job. Where does he go from here?

Failure symptoms:
- Nobody buys the product
- Nobody will fund it
- Nobody understands your uniqueness
- You never get out of the starting gate.

Test your idea

You have a great idea for a new product or service. You know it will be a huge success once it gets to market. So where do you start?

The first and most important thing is to test your idea. When the inventors of the Palm Pilot first got the idea, they created a wooden mockup that they carried around for months pretending to make entries and evaluating usefulness. It cost very little, but it was very effective. Apple's great ideas for the graphical user interface did not come from them, but from extensive research at Xerox Park. Apple simply brought them to a new user group and market. IBM can spend tens or even hundreds of thousands of dollars on market research but they can afford to. You need to have some low cost ways of evaluating your idea.

Friends, colleagues, mentors and the Internet are all good ways of testing the idea, but beware of the Mother Syndrome - "My mother thinks this is a great idea". When polling people it is most important to listen to what they are really saying. There are lots of signals that are optimistically misinterpreted or missed altogether. One of the worst things you can do is invest time and money in something and then not listen to those signals. This is one of the hardest things for entrepreneurs to do, but not doing it can be fatal.

Something you will see in this book over and over again is *record and measure everything!*

"Sometimes the key to a creative breakthrough is a good old fashioned whack on the side of the head."

Begin with using the Internet to assess the market size. Look for competing products or services, record why they are the same and identify what makes them different. Structured online queries often indicate numbers of hits or results and will provide you with an idea of the size of the market or problem.

For example, if you were writing a book on how to failure proof a business and wanted to assess the market and the competition, you might get the following results:

business book hits.................213,000,000 results
books on business failures.........254,000 results
relevant, non-repetitive books.....10 results
(many results being articles, reviews, booksellers and repeats)

When your business or service is the object of an online search, it is imperative that you are found quickly. All the 10 relevant books appear on the first Google web page indicating that they are well positioned.

From your initial search it looks like there is an opportunity because many of them have a single focus and are good references for the subject area. To sell your book however, you must find some way of getting to market and getting noticed.

There is free government research available to do your market sizing. If your target is a profession or a service, e.g. dentists, then the online Yellow Pages may be a good source. In addition, local municipal governments offer low cost CDs of demographic and business data. Another source can be local Chambers of Commerce. There will be no limit to sources of sizing your market potential, but remember sales volume is a combination of the size of the market, the price *(see Chapter 7 for pricing strategies)* and positioning on the traditional product introduction curve.

You need to look at the cost of building or offering your product or service. Don't forget that parts may be cheap, but service, warranty, returns, and distribution costs may have to be added to keep afloat *(see Chapter 4 on cash management)*.

Once you have a handle on the potential market, you must be realistic about how much of the market you can get and how quickly. This is an area where many people fail. They underestimate the time it will take to introduce a product and the potential barriers to entry they may encounter. Throwing money at problems to make them go away is not always successful and in most cases, you won't have that luxury.

"Business is lousy. Maybe I should have done more market research first."

Throughout your research you will make many assumptions about the market, product, competition, etc. An assumption is basically your best knowledge about a subject that is backed by evidence. Document them and test them constantly. They can be changed as events change and there may be alternative assumptions.

EXAMPLE

Based on research into trade press and talking with customers, you learn that the competition will introduce a new product in 6 months. The new product will be priced 25% below your product. You put a plan in place to reduce your price 1 month before. Now, are you prepared to act?

You may have to choose a method of getting to the market at a lower cost and perhaps in a slower time frame. This could be starting with Internet sales or a home based business until you develop your initial market.

All this information is necessary if you require any outside funding. The more facts you have now, the better your chances are for getting the funding you need. You will use it to build your business presentations and plans. Remember to record everything. You have paid for the information and proof of concept with your time and money so don't lose it.

Once you have collected ample information, sit down and write a business plan *(see Appendix for an outline)*. It will help organize your thoughts and presentations and more importantly, help secure additional funding. It is crucial that you are able to explain your idea in a chart or paragraph within a one-minute timeframe. You must be able to articulate the product or service as follows:

- The Problem… one or two short sentences
- The Primary Market… one sentence
- Your Solution… one or two short sentences
- The Benefit to the Investor… one short sentence
- Ask for the commitment then shut up and wait for the response! [1]***

If you do not choose to follow this simple formula, you are in for failure number one and you haven't even started yet!

*** *This is sales 101, but I can't count the number of times I've seen entrepreneurs talk themselves out of a deal simply by continuing to sell when they haven't heard the prospects' position, objections and intent.*

During this process, start to collect a board of advisors. This may be work colleagues, university professors and business leaders in several fields. You may be surprised at how many people will say yes to someone who is enthusiastically promoting his or her product. Consider the range of skills you might need including; finance, technical, logistics, general management, etc. Be prepared to offer some form of compensation such as options, shares or simply reimbursing for expenses.

Sample Product/Service Assessment Matrix*

Try the assessment matrix* provided with an honest ranking of your product or service. It is important to put yourself in the mind of a potential investor or customer to get a realistic assessment of your product or service. It would be even better to get one or more of your advisors to do the assessment to get a clearer picture of your potential to receive funding and ultimately sales. The items in the evaluation are explained below:

Note: If you cannot come up with a score of at least 60, then go back to the drawing board before talking to potential investors!

START WITH A GOOD IDEA

ITEM	WEIGHT	RANGE	SCORE	SCORING CRITERIA
A. Is the product or service function and benefit easily described or understood?	20	0 to 20		Complex=0 Complex/Compelling=5 Simple/Compelling=20
B. Is the industry a growth industry?	10	0 to 10		No growth=0 Slow growth=5 High growth=10
C. Do you trust the people who are doing the estimates; do they have a successful track record?	15	-5 to 15		Some question=-5 No track record=0 Good track record=15
D. Is the technology new?	5	-5 to 5		Bleeding edge=-5 New=0 Advanced=5
E. Where is it in the adoption cycle?	10	-5 to 10		Early=-5 Late=-5 Leading growth=10
F. Are there barriers to entry in the market (e.g. Patents)	5	-10 to 5		Major incumbents=-10 No barriers=0 Owned patents/skills=5
G. Can you accomplish the launch with existing skills? Can you hire the skills?	5	-5 to 5		Difficult=-5 Easy=0 In-house=5
H. Do you have a clear idea of who and how to market to?	10	0 to 10		Market is identifiable=0 Clear plan to buyer=10
I. Is the time to breakeven short or long?	20	-10 to 20		Greater than 3 years=-10 2 to 3 years=-5 Less than 2 years=5 to 10 Less than one year=15 to 20
Bonus Points:	10	0 to 10		Gross Margin GT 50%=10 Net Profit GT 10%=5
Total	110	>60		

Assessment Item Description

A. Simplicity - It is important to be able to describe your products function and benefits in simple and compelling terms. Identify how you and your investors are going to make money. A nuclear reactor is a complex piece of technology but in its simplest terms, it heats water to drive turbines to produce KWH of electricity at fraction of the cost of the alternatives.

B. Growth - If the industry is growing then it is much easier to take some market share. Growth will also hide a lot of other ills. Remember when the tide comes in, all ships will rise.

C. Trust - After gaining an understanding of your product/service, sharp investors will look you in the eye and ask some tough questions to determine whether or not you can deliver and how committed you are to the success of the product (both morally and financially). Everybody starts somewhere so if you don't have a good track record, your partners and advisors absolutely must have one.

D. Technology - This is a question of risk. If the product or service uses a *'bleeding edge'* technology, it may seem like an advantage but more often than not, it is a liability. When stuff goes wrong it may be expensive to fix.

E. Adoption Cycle - If you are dealing with early adopters, they may pay a high price to be first, but you also need a plan for how to move your product through the adoption cycle.

F. Barriers to Entry - On the plus, side if you have a new product with few entrenched competitors and it is protected by patents or proprietary processes, you have a good chance of success. If there are large entrenched competitors who have brands, patents or simply market share, you are in for a fight. Ask yourself how quickly will it take for others to catch up.

G. **Skills** - If you already have the key skills to accomplish your goals, great. If you can hire them quickly, go for it. But if the market for the skills you need is tight, the risks and costs go up.

H. **Market** - If you have the names and addresses of all your early clients, you are in good shape. If you have to find them or they have to find you, then you need to think about the most effective and efficient methods for getting to the potential clients.

I. **Breakeven** - In today's fast moving world, 3 years is a long time and risk goes up exponentially. If you are more than a year and a half before seeing a profit, you better have an incredibly compelling case to make for the product or service.

J. **Bonus Points** - If you have a valid and independently assessed product cost model *(see Chapter 4)*, you may add up to 10 additional points. The reason for this is that a large gross margin or a healthy (honest) net profit can cover for other mistakes.

* *Note: I use this matrix when evaluating projects or businesses for viability. The weightings may be different (explicit or implicit) for other evaluators or potential funders. Try to understand where they may be coming from before moving forward with your proposal. As an independent check, watch the TV programs Dragon's Den and Shark Tank. What they assess as important is consistent with the above matrix.*

EXAMPLE

A. IPS Automation (now Photon Dynamics) developed and manufactured alignment equipment for the computer monitor industry. The product was complex but the function and benefits could be simply described to a potential client. The business case was compelling in an industry with constant margin pressures **(15 points)**.

B. The industry had high growth and competitive penetration was low **(10 Points)**.

C. The CEO was a serial entrepreneur and there was a strong management team **(15 Points)**.

D. The technological base was sound, but the application was bleeding edge and complex to implement **(-5 Points)**.

E. The product was early in the adoption cycle and while there were some spec orders to mitigate risk, it was still a year or two from an accepted or "must have" technology **(-5 Points)**.

F. There were a few low-tech competitors, but IPS had significant intellectual property **(5 Points)**.

G. There were skills in house and more needed to be hired but were readily available **(5 Points)**.

H. The market was highly identifiable and IPS knew the names and locations of all major potential clients. Since a typical sale averaged $250,000, the sales model was direct sales it just required expense money to get to them **(10 Points)**.

I. Breakeven for the company was 1.5 to 2 years **(10 Points)**.

J. Bonus: The product gross margin was larger than 50% **(10 Points)**.

Total: 70 Points
(Results: IPS went through 3 rounds of successful funding)

CASE STUDY

IBM wanted to compete directly with the sale of PC Clones, but its corporate cost structure was too high to be effective. The solution – we set up a separate company structured very much like a clone manufacturer. It was a simple idea. Our differentiation was IBM quality standards and unique design. While there were many startup problems it was successful in a couple of ways. First, it allowed us to compete head to head with companies like Dell and secondly, we learned a lot about the low cost market. Ambra Computer Corp. was eventually closed down but the lessons learned were put to good use in the IBM Consumer Division. We totally restructured the division to make it much more profitable. The key was to use a totally different business model than IBM had used in the past. Traditionally, IBM was a return on revenue model but in the PC industry where margins were thin, we needed to use a return on assets model similar to many big box stores. We outsourced everything, utilized global logistics and inventory planning, and paid our suppliers in 45 days. We treated them fairly as partners and we collected from our dealers in 30 days. As it turned out, if you don't own much in the way of assets, a one or two percent profit can yield a very high return.

ROADRUNNER TECHNOLOGIES

Bob went online and found some similar products to the one he had planned. All of them were seriously deficient in the functionality needed to meet potential customer requirements and none seem to be making it big, in what appeared to be a big market.

Bob went to some local companies and former business associates, and interviewed them to uncover what was required to meet their needs. It was surprisingly easy to get in to see these key players. One even said that they might be willing to place a modest order if he got it going. He also went to the local government and got access to their business database. From there he was able to estimate the number of similar potential customers and then scale it up for his immediate region. This gave him a pretty good idea that he had a potential winner. Bob wondered how could he differentiate himself from his competitors and convince clients of his product's value.

CHAPTER 2
Get your positioning right

"It's the first company to build the mental position that has the upper hand, not the first company to make the product. IBM didn't invent the computer; Sperry Rand did. But IBM was the first to build the computer position in the prospect's mind."

Al Ries

Failure Symptoms:
- You can't explain your uniqueness to customers and potential investors
- Your staff is not sure of the essence of the product or service and so delivers conflicting messages
- You have conflicting communications to potential customers. (E.g. "We are the cheapest and the highest quality." You can be the price leader in high quality products, but not the cheapest.)

- Everyone is confused about what you stand for and they go somewhere else.

From a marketing perspective, getting your positioning right is the most important thing you can do. Positioning is the foundation and branding is the building. Positioning is new but branding is as old as Greek vases. There are many good books on positioning written by Trout and Ries. Any one of them will give you a more in depth understanding of positioning. My favorite is the *"22 Immutable Laws of Marketing"*, which over the course of my career I believe I violated most of them.

Positioning is:
- A set of key messages summarizing the benefits to the customer
- A unique statement for a company, product or service
- What defines what a company represents in a market and vs. competition
- What are we, what do we do well and what others think we do well.

Your positioning statement must be *believable*. A one-person, full service shop may be the best in the world, but how would you convince anyone of it.

Your positioning statement must be *meaningful,* not only to you but to your target customer. For example, a cable provider who positions oneself as having the fastest service will have an audience with those customers who download a lot. A meaningful positioning statement is *"Avis - We try harder."* At the time it was developed, they were not the biggest player in the automotive rental industry so this statement made a connection and became meaningful to their customers.

Your positioning statement must be *unique*. Dentists often struggle with how to make themselves standout. The key is to narrow the focus. For example, full service, specialized or child friendly.

Your positioning statement must be *consistent* and you must walk the talk. Imagine if you walked up to an Avis counter and they aren't trying harder. You start to doubt the company, its' employees and services. You can't be both the cheapest and the best quality. It's simply not believable. In addition, your company cannot be known for one thing and easily introduce a product for an opposing market. IBM experienced this problem, as they were traditionally known for large corporate solutions. Big Blue had its share of struggles when they introduced a personal computer.

Positioning is for the long term and if you get it right, it will last. It takes a long time to set a new positioning and even longer to change your positioning as we found out with the IBM PC. Take the example of Tide®. They have had the same positioning for 100 years - *"Tide gets clothes clean"*. They no longer use the words as their slogan but go to their website and you will see the impact of their positioning.

Your positioning statement must be *enduring*. Volvo has been well positioned as safe and reliable family transportation since it was introduced. Recently they have been trying to reposition themselves as a performance company. What is the first thing that comes to mind when you think of Volvo? Exactly.

There are different approaches to positioning including:
- **Product attributes** - If your products have a reputation for safety like Volvo or quality like Honda, then these should be the core of your positioning. However, you need to be careful that you do not focus on something too narrow or too transitory. This is also true in company, product and brand naming. Being too specific means you are in for a long process of repositioning. An example of a successful company who has done this is Arm and Hammer Baking Soda. Fewer people bake these days so it was a long and difficult survival tactic on their part.
- **Benefit or problem solution** - Again, Arm and Hammer is the best example of this positioning. They are not a baking product, but an odor solution. After a long battle to change their positioning you now see the product in toothpaste and deodorant.
- **Specific use -** A milk equipment company like Delaval… not exactly a household name, but well known in the industry.
- **Against a competitor -** This is very tricky because if you say, "We are not them!" you actually reinforce their positioning. However, you can decide to position yourself to a market that they do not cover, such as quality or service. This may be an effective way to introduce your company or product into a market dominated by a larger competitor. This is Chairman Mao's strategy - *When superior, attack. When equal, form alliances and when outnum-*

bered, use guerilla warfare. You will need to do competitive positioning anyway to test your uniqueness, but make sure that you can prove your positioning and that it is believable. You cannot say that you are the largest supplier of quality products when there is a large competitor, but you can call yourself the quality leader. Again, the best example of this is the *"Avis – We try harder"* campaign.

"My team has created a very innovative solution, but we're still looking for a problem to go with it."

So how do you develop your positioning?
- List the wants and needs the product may satisfy
- Identify competitors – primary and secondary

- Learn how their customers and yours perceive competitors
- Learn how your competitors customers and yours perceive you
- Identify gaps and opportunities that your company can satisfy
- Develop positioning to create intended perception that you define. This is not a slogan but how you will define your whole offering - your product, your service, your people and the target customer.

Remember it's the customer's perception, not yours, that counts! It is not a matter of right and wrong, it's a matter of win and lose. If you argue with a customer's perception, rightly or wrongly, you will lose every time!

So why have I focused so much on positioning? Because if you get it right your funding, promotion and even your employee management, becomes much easier. Here is one last insight on the topic: Entrepreneurs and sales people have a habit of wanting to change things after a month or so. If your positioning is working for you, do not do anything to change or damage it!

For more details on extending these thoughts to branding, read *"Managing Brand Equity"* by David Aaker, and Positioning: The Battle for Your Mind 20th Anniversary Edition by Al Ries and Jack Trout.

CASE STUDY

I reviewed a company called DOTCOM2000. A great name if the dotcom bubble didn't break and the year was 1998. Unfortunately, it was 2001 and the name gave an instant positioning that no investor would touch with a 10-foot pole. What was worse, the products they proposed had nothing to do with their name or their mission statement and had little relation to one another. They struggled but never got out of the gate and in spite of some good ideas; they constantly fought their initial positioning.

After leaving IBM, I joined a startup called Image Processing Systems (IPS). Using imaging technology, they made quality test and adjustment equipment for the computer monitor and TV industry. Their positioning was the best imaging technology solutions for quality assurance. While the market was well defined, in two years they were recognized as the technology leaders and by far not the cheapest. They solved a customer problem cost effectively and they dominated the industry. Only when they tried to go outside this positioning did some problems occur.

The message of these two companies is simple; 1) stick to a positioning as long as it's working and 2) you can never easily explain to a customer that you aren't who they think you are!

ROADRUNNER TECHNOLOGIES

Bob developed a positioning statement that focused on his products unique features and the high service level he planned to offer. He developed his elevator pitch, wrote a 3 page executive summary and a complete business plan. The key part of the business plan focused on cash requirements. Bob then set up his website describing the company and the products. He also incorporated as Roadrunner Technologies Ltd.

Bob went to some former clients and business associates to develop a board of advisors. He and a key engineer (working part-time) built a prototype funded largely out of his savings. Bob brought one of his former co-workers as a partner (who had also been given a severance package and who had sales and marketing experience) to provide more depth to the team. Bob enlisted a small group of potential employees that would be hired if he got additional funding. The team looked impressive on paper. He went back to his potential clients and got a promise of enough provisional orders to get them started. Now he needed some cash injection to fund the final development and production.

CHAPTER 3
Securing your funding

"These days, it may be easier to raise startup money than it was during the boom. No, it doesn't seem that way. But that's a perception promulgated by precarious or now deceased startups. The companies founded two or three years ago have been struggling with the assumption that follow-on investments would be as easy to get as the initial funding, ... They're not getting the follow-on funding, and so they're telling people that VCs don't want to spend. We do, but more on the traditional companies missed during the dot-com bubble."

- Geoffrey Moore

Failure Symptoms:
- You run out of money needed to operate
- You lose control of the company
- You wind up with a lot of personal debt

Rule #1 for survival: Cash is king and there is no Rule # 2!

If you have already started your business skip over this section temporarily and go to the section on Alternate Funding. The alternative funding approach should always be the default.

The key point to remember and you will not want to hear this, but the days of other people's money are gone! You need to make sure you have all your skin in the game. If you think you've got the perfect idea and somebody else will pay for it, forget about it. That may have happened in the tech boom (bubble), but no lender or investor worth their salt, will give you a nickel for something if your heart, your house, your family and friends and your first born are not on the hook for. The reasoning is obvious. The lender wants to make sure that you have more to lose than they do and that translates into commitment. So with this in mind, what do you need to secure funding?

First off, you need is a valid reason. For the record, here are some of the wrong reasons for seeking outside funding:

1. *I need to get other peoples' money so I can pay myself better.* Forget other peoples' money except maybe rich Aunt Thelma.
2. *I need to go public to expand my business.* Going public too early can be a significant mistake for an emerging business. It brings in all sorts of additional people to control and report to like the Securities and Exchange Commission (SEC), Venture Capitalists and the Board of Directors, not to mention the press and investors. In addition,

it is often a higher cost of borrowing and be careful of the fine print with the venture capitalist; you may wind up on the out. Going public is a good alternative way of funding a growing business, but it needs to be thought through carefully and it is neither cheap nor quick.
3. *I need to take money out of the business.* It doesn't matter what your reasons are this doesn't work. Do well and you will get paid.
4. *My business is in trouble and I need a bailout.* You may have to do this, but don't expect to have much left when you come through it unless you have a proven track record of seasonality and all you need is to bridge a few months. Plan so this doesn't happen again.

Here are some of the right reasons:
1. *I need to expand my business.* If you can show a growing and realistic market backed by realistic projections of profitability this will work.
2. *I have a new market and the time to capitalize is now.*
3. *I have some big new contracts and I need bridge financing to get me to delivery.*
4. *I have a new product and the launch costs require some bridge financing.*
5. *I need to hire a couple of additional key people to help expand the business.*

Regardless of your reasons for seeking funding, investors will want the same basic information.

People vs. Projections

Most sources of financing tend to put more faith in the people involved in the business and their track records. While projections can be important, they are usually discounted unless they are heavily backed by orders - conditional and otherwise. A backlog can be factored in and combined with a delivery track record, which may be based on past shipments. Customer testimonials are also valuable.

Business Plan

The importance of writing a business plan is primarily to ensure you can answer all the questions you will be asked to support your funding requests. Don't get too fancy with your business plan because most investors will only read the summary, source and use of funds then look at the projections. *(See Appendix for a template).* Having said this, when you are before the potential funders you must know all the numbers off the top of your head. Market size, cost, scalability, competition, market prices, skill sets and much more, needs to be readily available for you to respond to any question without hesitation. "I'll get back to you," rarely works. This is not only part of building your credibility, but also essential to your survival as the business evolves.

Failing hard evidence supporting the potential for success, you must present the people in your organization who have a reputation for developing or running companies like yours. This will include your Board of Directors and Advisors.

Note: Governments have put a significant liability on Directors. The people you want may be reluctant unless there is trust and full disclosure. When directors are difficult to sign up, consider advisors and revamping director financing as well.

So what are investors looking for in the people that they will fund?
- The skills to do the job backed by past experience.
- The people must be committed to the overall success of the company by being heavily invested and minimally compensated. You will be well reimbursed when you are successful, but the financial institution does not want to be the only one holding the bag if the worst should happen.
- On TV programs such as "Dragon's Den" or "Shark Tank", potential investors are pitched ideas and business plans by entrepreneurs that require funding. The Investors were asked what was the common denominator in approving funding. Loosely translated, the answer given by Investment Banker Kevin O'Reilly, who stars in the show was, "First they have to articulate the idea in the first couple of minutes and second, we have to believe they can execute the plan."

These resumes may be the most important thing you prepare to get your funding. And remember when doing your presentations, you may need to involve your *Royal Smart Person,* but make sure that you rehearse and that he or she knows when to shut up. Too many deals die on the table from too much talking.

So now you're at the stage where you have exhausted friends and family, so with the business plan, positioning, projections, resumes and presentation, where do you go next?

- **Banks** - While banks generally have the reputation of only lending money to those who don't need it, in tougher times the process may be even more difficult. That said it is likely to be your lowest cost of borrowing. Be prepared to put up collateral in addition to having a good story. You will likely need a revolving line of credit to cover the seasonality in any business and the banks are the best place to get this. They will want to see a strong track record before they help you.

- **Investors** - Other than rich Aunt Thelma, investors are likely to come directly or indirectly from your business associates. Set up a Board of Advisors to help you. Remember that investors are in this for the return so be prepared to give up a generous piece of the action. I have seen many deals go south because the principal is far too greedy and they never get the funding they need. Most smart investors want the principals to own more than half of the company because this ensures that you are committed and that they will get the return they need. They don't typically want to run the company, but they do insist on reasonable reporting and potentially board seats.
- **Alliances & Buyouts** - If you have an operating company with a killer product, you may find that both related companies and competitors are willing to finance your operations, typically for a controlling interest. Usually they will want the principals to stay on for a period of time so compensation can be quite lucrative. If your company has grown beyond your skill or interest level, this can be an ideal solution and companies may approach you first! Smart entrepreneurs realize that they are often serial entrepreneurs and not big company presidents.
- **Venture Capitalists** - There are a number of companies who engage in funding activities in exchange for a share

of the company. They range from Angel Capital companies to Operation Funding companies. They tend not to provide capital directly, but engage in private placement with a stable of investors. They expect to make their money by dividends back to investors or a shared exit strategy based on the company being acquired or going public in the future. They will often charge for the expenses and in the case of a public offering, the amount may be quite large. The expenses include lawyers, consultants and prospectus production.
- **Factoring companies** - If you have large orders for the immediate future, this may be a source of financing by signing over all or part of the future revenue from the transaction to a factoring company. This may be necessary but often the interest rates and terms are steep.

Alternate sources of funding
- **Your receivables** - Nobody likes to collect money. Actually, let's make that nobody likes the process of collecting money, but it must be done. Many of your clients by plan will stretch out their payments to you. Large clients do this as a standard practice to pay in 45 or 60 days. They often are very sensitive the survival needs of a small business so present your case to get paid early. For smaller and intermediate clients, offer terms known as trade credit, and cost it in. An example is the 2/10, net 30, which is a 2% discount if you pay in 10 days. The bottom line is to get on the phone and collect. Don't depend on your sales force to do this as it can cause undue stress, affect client relationships and their overall focus.

SECURING YOUR FUNDING

- **Negotiate payments** - Your suppliers may be willing to negotiate terms if you can show that it is needed for operation but not out of desperation. As long as they are confident that they will get paid, they are usually flexible because a forced bankruptcy is not good for anyone. In addition, it is very common in retail to offer floor financing. You may also find terms available on volume, and quick turn around transactions. Just ask and see what the options are. With respect to volume deals, make sure you can sell the product. It may sound obvious, but all too often a sweetheart deal turns out to require the product be sold at a loss because they have no hope of meeting the volumes for the deal!

"Our terms are net 30 days. If you don't pay after 20 days, we come after you with a net!"

- **Expense and cash management** - For every dollar you save, you're saving the additional cost of borrowing it. Not to mention the time and energy required locating and acquiring that financing. Driving an expensive car and having a fancy office might feed your ego, but they add to your expenses and may not be viewed positively by clients and investors. However, if you have to spend money on something that is needed, it is better to do it with "before tax" dollars than "after tax" dollars. A word of caution - expensing items that are not business related can expose your company to a government audit.

Government programs - Federal, State, Provincial and Regional Governments all compete for the jobs your company has created and may create in the future. Such programs typically target specific sectors like new energy technology, problems such as youth employment, and R&D or modernization investment. It's surprising the number of companies who leave government money on the table out of ignorance or laziness. There are so many programs and agencies available that you will need to research them yourself using the Internet and advisors. They vary by country, state and even timing. To illustrate the breadth of programs available, I have briefly summarized some of the programs available in Canada at the time of printing. (Source: Small Business Finance Centre (http://www.grants-loans.org)).

Grants and subsidies (one-time & renewable) - When you receive this money you don't have to pay it back. It's yours to use under the terms of the grant. The federal and provincial governments know that it's tough for small businesses like yours to bring new products to market, make your company more efficient, or hire employees. So they provide billions of dollars a year to aid Canadian product innovation and grow small businesses. There are also subsidies like hire a student, a new graduate or an immigrant.

In Canada, there are currently 39 Federal and 57 Provincial programs available, offering between $1,500 - $500,000 worth of funding.

Low-interest or no-interest loans - While a grant is obviously an ideal source of government funding, you have an even greater chance of accessing government programs that provide financing for small businesses through loans. So if you've made the rounds of the banks and been shown the door, don't give up.

There are currently 83 Federal and 82 Provincial low or no-interest loan programs available, offering between $1,500 - $10 million worth of funding.

Tax refunds or tax credits - Getting money is obviously beneficial. But not having to pay it in the first place amounts to the same thing, and can even be better. The government offers a variety of programs that decrease your tax burden, including programs that provide a lower tax rate for small businesses, award tax credits for hiring eligible apprentices, and provide investment tax credits (ITCs) for qualified expenditures in R&D.

There are currently 11 Federal and 23 Provincial programs available, offering between $3,500 - 2 million worth of funding.

Government insurance against business risks - For low and sometimes no premiums, you can have the government insure your business against various risks, providing valuable assurances to financial institutions and making it easier for you to borrow.

For example, Export Development Canada (EDC) will insure your accounts receivable, covering your full book of business for up to 90 percent of your losses against such risks if customers are refusing to pay.

There are currently 7 Federal and 8 Provincial programs available, offering between $20,000 - 10 million worth of funding.

Government relocation incentives - If you're willing (or eager) to move to a new facility or even a new province, you may find incentives that make the move that much more attractive.

There are currently 7 Federal and 6 Provincial programs available, offering between $5,000 - $500,000 worth of funding.

"Today we are introducing a new simplified tax code: Send us all of your money and we'll send back whatever we don't use."

What not to do:
Borrow from the government by not paying taxes - This sounds obvious, but it happens all too often. You deduct taxes from your employee paychecks and don't pay them to the government, or you collect but don't pay sales, value added or other business taxes on time. When you are desperate, it may sound attractive, but it also may be illegal. The cost of repayment to the government borders on usury and almost never works. In most jurisdictions, the directors or officers are personally liable to the government for repayment.

Borrow from "Vulture Capitalists" - Vulture Capitalists are a particular form of venture capitalists. The difference is in the fine print. Their motivation is to get you going and then take control of the company when it is about to achieve success. The terms may be good up front but the performance targets are often unachievable and when you don't make them, you give up something huge. They appear to be flexible as the company progresses, but at each point you give up something else until there is almost nothing left for you. Be aware, they are out there so proceed with caution. The terms and costs might make the mafia blush.

CASE STUDY

IPS started on borrowed premises with the principals mortgaged to the hilt, living off pizza and credit cards. This just went to show that the principals were committed. IPS went through several rounds private and public funding. We had a solid product with some on spec orders but they needed cash flow insurance because of their long delivery cycle. Early on they factored some orders at a very high cost, just to get them going. The real secret to getting this money was a very charismatic CEO, who was a successful serial entrepreneur and who could succinctly articulate IPS' needs. People listened and put money into the company.

For some operating cash IPS used a Canadian Government program called IRAP (Industrial Research Assistance Program) specifically geared to the development of products for export in targeted industries. While it is not a grant, but rather a repayable loan, it is off the books because it is only repaid out of product revenues. In addition, an export development program was used to underwrite orders with long lead times. This combined with prudent cash management, allowed IPS to grow the company from $2 million to

$30 million and to become Exporter of the Year. From there IPS sought out awards and heavily promoted itself to get additional help when needed from banks, government, or private and public markets.

ROADRUNNER TECHNOLOGIES

To get started, Bob secured a line of credit with his house as collateral. His partner matched these funds. While he did not get any cash from his provisional orders, there was a written statement of progress payments. He was able to secure a government grant and hire new graduates. With this news he convinced an Angel Investor to kick in additional cash based on a progress schedule. He had to give up 25% of the company and if he did not make certain milestones, he might lose control of the company. This was the best deal he could get. He was now ready to rent facilities, hire staff and procure materials. Roadrunner Technologies signed the deal and opened for business.

CHAPTER 4
Cash management

"A penny saved is a penny earned."
Benjamin Franklin

Failure symptoms:
- *You run out of cash in a "successful" business*
- *You can't take action until after you are in trouble*
- *You don't really know what your sales are*
- *You don't really know if you are making a profit*

This chapter focuses on a three fundamental management programs you must put in place in order not to fail:
- Cash forecasting
- Sales forecasting
- Product/Service cost monitoring.

"I won't be needing you to deliver our quarterly financial report. I've hired a blues band."

Cash forecasting

Cash forecasting is key to the survival of your business. More businesses fail for lack of cash flow than for lack of profit. In fact, when you look at the spectacular failures of large successful businesses like Ames and Circuit City, a common element is the pursuit of growth for growth's sake. In a small and medium business this is usually an instant death, not the slow wasting away as experienced in large corporations.

Note: Another thing to be mindful of is elephant hunting. This simply means going after large orders in some very large businesses. This may bring instant success, but be sure you have the cash reserves to go after this type of customer. Remember, elephants are very easy to see but hard to bring down.

When planning the short- or long-term funding requirements of a business, it is more important to forecast the likely cash requirements than to project profitability. Profit is the difference between sales and costs within a specified period, and the generation of a profit does not necessarily guarantee business survival.

Sales, costs and profits do not necessarily coincide in time with their associated cash inflows and outflows. While a sale may have been secured and the goods delivered, the related payment may be deferred as a result of terms or collection issues. At the same time payments that must be made to suppliers or payroll, require cash, and cash must also be invested in replenishing depleted stocks or the purchase of new equipment.

The net result is that cash receipts often follow cash payments and although profits may be reported, the business may experience a short-term cash deficit. For this reason it is essential to forecast cash flows as well as project likely profits.

You must read and understand the cash flow reports at least once a week!   Schedule it on your calendar and do not accept any excuses for it not being done.

The following is a simplified example that illustrates the timing differences between profits and cash flows:

INCOME STATEMENT		PROFIT		
Sales ($000)		75		
Costs ($000)		65		
Profit ($000)		10		
Cash flows relating to Month 1	Month 1	Month 2	Month 3	Total
Receipts from sales ($000)	20	35	20	75
Payments to suppliers, etc. ($000)	40	20	5	65
Net cash flow ($000)	(20)	15	15	10
Cumulative net cash flow ($000)	(20)	(5)	10	10

This chart shows the cash associated with the reported profit from sales is spread over 3 months and will not appear until the end of the period. So there will be a serious cash shortfall experienced during the first and second months.

What must be added to the above is available cash on hand either through past sales or line of credit. In the previous example, a $25,000 line of credit at the start of the period will result in $35,000 in available cash for the next sales cycle.

As you can see it does not have to be rocket science but you do have to forecast revenues and payments. These can be different from costs because of timing when calculating the net cash requirements. Off the shelf tools or your own spreadsheets can help achieve this. The toughest part of cash management is forecasting. You'll notice that I did not say accurate forecasting, which is an oxymoron.

Revenues

Sales forecasts - you need to get dependable sales forecasts that are turned into payments based on your sales terms or history, which are not necessarily the same. There is more on this later.

Other revenue: interest, royalties, government grants, collections and refunds - all are important to track when managing cash flow.

Cash outlays

Salaries - Salaries and commissions are important cash outflows since they can seldom be deferred without creating major problems.

Supplier payments - Suppliers require a schedule of payments so these can be easily predicted in connection with sales. The challenge is when you have long lead-time components and have to combine them with sales forecasts and manufacturing uncertainties. This is a time for renegotiations if you cannot meet your cash requirements without changes to your payment terms. Having a cash flow plan can help you work through this.

Expenses - Rent, heat, utilities, sales and marketing expenses, major travel outlays and special events also need to be planned and timing determined for when they NEED to be paid. If you don't time the payments right, you may find yourself in trouble.

Whether you buy a program, use a spreadsheet or have your CFO produce it, you need to prepare weekly statement of cash requirements and review it once a week until you are comfortable with it. Once the process is operating well, the CFO or controller can manage it weekly, but you must be able to review it on demand, at a minimum of once a month. If you don't do this, your chances of survival are in the hands of the gods.

Sales forecasting

This is one of the most difficult things for principals to get their minds around. Firstly, they tend to be optimists by nature and secondly, sales reps and agents hate having to forecast. Payments and sales are difficult to synchronize, especially when lead times are long for both supplies and manufacturing. You may not enjoy the synchronization process but it must be done!

Both principals and sales reps tend to have a binary estimate of sales depending on the last sales call. It is either 5% or 95%. Both numbers are usually wrong. First, you must force a sales forecast and then you must discount the revenue associated with the forecast. How this is done is very straight forward, but it must be modified according to your business model and sales cycle.

Every sales process is exactly the same, only the timing is different:
- Awareness
- Liking
- Preference
- Commitment
- Order

An excellent book that shows how to move prospects through the sales cycle, particularly in the Internet world, is "*Permission Marketing*" by Seth Godin, one of the Gurus responsible for the success of Yahoo.

The time for the sales cycle depends on the product, whether the customers are early or late adopters and the impact of the decision *(cost vs. value)*. It may take hours, weeks or months to go through the complete cycle. That is why you need lots of customers at the early stages to ensure that some make it through to order. The point of the sales cycle is to understand how many potential customers are needed at the start *(suspects)* to turn a percentage into prospects and then a percentage of those, into customers.

As an example, if you have a small ticket item and decide to use direct mail (a very expensive approach today), you can expect around a 1% response rate so you will need thousands of mail outs to generate any reasonable amount of sales. You may improve this to 3 to 5% if you have a call out process, which can work for certain products. You might only convert 10 or 20% of these into actual sales. You must take the delays into account for your cash flow model such as, paying for the mail out today and getting some orders in month 1 and more in month 2. The Internet has an advantage in that it allows access to millions of suspects, but the trick is finding them.

Since I cannot give you exact guidelines for your specific industry, why even talk about this segment? Well, if you can't forecast sales, then you can't forecast cash flow, and you run the risk of flying blind. Sales reps must report on calls, contacts, interests, presentations, proposals and orders. If they do not give you this information then you cannot develop your forecast model. Therefore, it must be done. I have provided a model I have worked with before that illustrates how this may be accomplished.

Assume you have a database of 1000 prospects and it takes 3 months from interest to shipment and 1 month to deliver. The phases are as follows:

- Qualification involves ensuring that a particular individual has the interest and means needed to become a potential customer. Assign no value, but make sure you keep the funnel full.
- Presentation is the initial sales pitch detailing the benefits of the product or service being offered for sale. A presentation is made to 100 customers in month 1. Value 5% (generally 5-10%).
- Proposal is the introduction of sales terms into the fold. Value 10%. A proposal is made to 50 customers.
- Negotiation is the attempt to establish a mutual agreement of sales terms. Value 40%. Negotiations with 20 customers.
- Close is the finalization of the sale and end of business. Value 90%. Ten customers place orders.
- Delivery is the receipt of the final product by the purchasing party. Value 100%. Deliveries are made to 9 customers.
- Evaluation involves follow up with the customer and possible introduction to future sales leads. This may reduce the value of a delivered order.

This is an overly simplified model but it can be a very effective planning tool. The results on sales might be as follows:

	# CUSTOMERS	VALUE	MONTH 1	MONTH 2	MONTH 3	MONTH 4
Qualification	1000	0%				
Presentation	100	5%				5
Proposal	50	10%			5	
Negotiations	20	40%			8	
Orders	10	95%		9.5		
Delivery	9	100%	9			
Sales			9	9.5	13	5

Since you roll this every month (or week), you can see how you can develop an order pattern. In this case, you may do it by customer name. You can conclude that you need to be making more calls and more presentations otherwise month 4 may be a little thin. You should not use sales reps opinions to change the probabilities more than a little. So if they say they are in negotiations and it's a 90 percent, maybe up the rule percentage for that deal to 45%. The worst that can happen here is that you may be a bit conservative and so may have to scramble on a few orders. You will get better over time.

A last note of caution set your sales compensation plan carefully. It is the guideline to the sales force and good sales people will follow it religiously to maximize their income. There are many ways to set up sales plan compensation. Some examples include a percentage of revenue, a percentage of profit or a percentage of gross margin. In addition, you can pay bonuses on products, customer types *(small vs. large)*, or specific industries. A particularly good plan is to bonus options and service contracts because there are often very high profit margins here. Two good examples of this are car dealers and electronics stores.

Most good sales reps are sales plan lawyers. They will very quickly figure out where the low hanging fruit is and how to best take advantage of the plan. If you set the plan right, account for it in your cost model, and a sales person makes more money than the president… good for him or her and good for you. If they are following the plan and you are getting the wrong results, it is your problem not theirs. You must renegotiate the plan, which is easiest at the end of a period.

Product cost models

I am constantly amazed at the number of companies that do not have realistic and tested cost/pricing models. When I worked at IBM in the PC division, I carried a cost model on my PDA that I used in supplier negotiations in Asia. This allowed me to instantly evaluate deal alternatives and make adjustments on the spot. This type of information can also be used in assessing volume sales deals or changes in terms for a deal. As an Operating Executive you need to know not only that you will make a profit but also where the profit is coming from.

CASE STUDY

A technology company made products in the 100 to 200 thousand-dollar range. They had revenues of $25 million a year. Their pricing was very simple. They uplifted the hardware cost by a factor of 3 and they had always shown a profit in the past. So what is wrong with this? First, this is a cost plus model for pricing, which often leaves money on the table if there is little competition. Secondly, most of their cost was in software development and support so the hardware cost uplift generated a profit by accident. As it turned out, they made a profit on most of their product lines but not as much as they thought on others. Some were not profitable at all. Where they really made their money was in service contracts and the profit margin here was very large. The problem was that they did not manage service as a business, but as a necessary evil. This company was lucky that they found this out before a change in the economy or competition forced them to make cuts. With a costing model, they know the impact of changes and know where to cut or focus on efficiency.

Most cost models are not very difficult to develop. Just make sure that you include all of your costs, both actual and amortized, in the model and that they balance, more or less, with the company balance sheet in the end. It can be done for a product, a service or a division, whatever makes sense. Also, remember that most costs do not increase linearly with volume.

For example, you may get a volume break that drops the average cost, but this break may also come with an increased risk of obsolescence and scrap. Some expenses have stepwise impacts on cost. When you are small, you cannot easily add a half a person to your service organization *(except with part time staff)* and so the cost allocation required may be much larger until you have an individual fully employed.

CASH MANAGEMENT

Here are some of the things to remember when developing cost models for a product business:

ITEM	COMMENTS
Average Selling Price	Some prefer the net average here
Average Discounts	Some prefer to track discounts
Net Average Selling Price	
Costs	
Product Component Costs	If you have major components where the price fluctuates. List them all separately, particularly in low-margin businesses
Manufacturing Overhead Contribution	Amortize
Specific Manufacturing Expenses	Assembly hours... this could include customization
Contracted Manufacturing Costs	Should be tracked separately for supplier evaluation
Shipping and Insurance	
Total Direct Costs	
Gross Margin	
Amortized Development Costs	
Amortized Obsolescence Costs	No doubt you will have some including scrap
Amortized Overheads	Building, admin, etc.
Selling Expenses	Includes salary, commissions and expenses (direct or amortized)
Amortized Marketing Expense	
Allocated Warranty Cost	You effectively purchase this from your service business
Other	There is always an other
Net Profit	

This may not be all, but it is a start. Be sure to track each of the costs to understand if they are realistic. If you start to get in trouble, say manufacturing quality issues, this is a good tool to evaluate the impact and the effect of corrective action.

Also, many of the choices are industry driven. For example the software industry deals with amortization differently than hard goods manufacturing. Review your competition and industry to understand what is common and perhaps more importantly, for benchmarking purposes. Some of the choices may be government/tax driven, but these are often not used except for calculating tax liabilities, and are occasionally one time or extraordinary items. Some become 'religious' choices and do not matter as long as you understand them.

By religious I mean how you or your accountant prefer to measure these items and there is no right or wrong, but they are usually argued to death.

If you are a service business, most of the line items hold, proportions just change. For example, a dentist still has components and contracted manufacturing (lab work); he just doesn't call them that. But the use principle is the same.

CASE STUDY

A company* that imported electronics sold mostly to chain stores came to an agreement with one of the big box stores to stock a combo TV/VCR. It was Christmas time and shipments were strong. The company booked the revenue and celebrated the year's achievements. Unfortunately, they forgot several principles about cash vs. revenue and did not account properly for returns. They also forgot that big box stores do not sell, they rent shelf space with long payment terms - usually 45 days, have an unlimited returns policy and take a share of the profit with very little risk. Towards the end of January, the company got a call from the big box purchaser saying they had a lot of customer returns and items still on the shelf to be returned to the company and would they come and pick them up! The results of a 20% return of product (most in open boxes) was quite significant since much of it had to be written off at a cost of more than the profit. The company teetered but weathered the storm with a hard lesson learned.

The lessons
1. Know your customer and their business model to properly put in place a costing model that takes into account returns and shelf inventory… and manage it.
2. Don't count your chickens before they hatch and reflect this in your cost and cash flow models.
3. Watch the store level inventory *(inventory management 101)* and make sure that you have a plan to take advantage of opportunities or manage threats. Remember, even if you have limited stock return terms, a store level

inventory of unsold product is still your problem and if you don't help the dealer out (e.g. run a promotion), it will impact future revenues.

* *I have not used the company names here because they are still in business and did not publish the facts beyond an accounting footnote.*

ROADRUNNER TECHNOLOGIES

One of the first things Bob did was to write down all of the key expenditures and the timeline. All this went into an Excel spreadsheet. Bob paid himself and his partners a modest salary and his engineer also became a partner. Bob developed an employee incentive plan to keep early cash costs down. He rented modest facilities with a short-term lease and an option on expansion. As he progressed to his first sales, he reviewed his cash flow statements weekly and he kept all of his stakeholders *(partners, bank and investors)* apprised of the progress monthly. Things were on right track and orders began to flow in.

CHAPTER 5
Process engineering is not just for big companies

"The proof of the pudding is in the eating."
Traditional English Proverb

"If you don't know where you're going, you're unlikely to end up there."
Forrest Gump

Failure Symptoms:
- *Customer satisfaction is low*
- *Lead times are long*
- *Inventories are high*
- *Response times are long*
- *Receivables are high.*

During the 1990's, process engineering and re-engineering was very popular among larger companies and have been very successful in helping them fix existing processes and create new ones. Many consulting firms have successful practices often based on market sector oriented process engineering.

So what is a process?
A business process is a method or system for achieving a commercial result. It begins with a customer's need and ends with a fulfullment of that need. Process oriented organizations break down the barriers of structural departments and try to avoid interdepartmental contention.

You can see by the second part why large organizations latched on to Business Process Re-engineering. They often have departments who defend interdepartmental lines and forget the basic purpose of the company. Small and intermediate businesses can ill afford this conflict and so it is generally stamped out quickly. However, I continue to be amazed at the number of companies who as they grow, forget that the business process begins with a customer's need and ends with customer need fulfillment.

So they expand without defining the basic processes to quickly answer questions like:

- Where is my order?
- When will it ship?
- How much is the invoice for?
- If I want to add something, what does it cost and when will I get it? *(Like tacking on an option or a service agreement that yields a high profit).*
- I have a problem can you help me?

Any business owner can tell you what the top ten questions are for their business. Write them down and define the process that is needed to meet customer expectations. It does not have to be sophisticated at the start. A well organized filing system or simple database software may suffice. Whatever you choose, you must ensure the process is enforced and that the data gets into the files. The big caution here is to make sure that you build your processes and systems for where you want to be, not where you are.

One company I worked with experienced explosive growth and implemented systems in an unplanned fashion. The end result was that none of the systems communicated with another and simple processes, like order tracking that worked so well on a smaller scale could not be effectively executed on a larger scale. Make sure you plan for growth consistent with your vision.

CASE STUDY
The situation

A large customer support center for a direct response marketing company was faced with major customer dissatisfaction and was being investigated by consumer advocates.

The wait time on the phones was pushing 45 minutes and the abandon rate was 95%. Order cancellation was high and employee moral was low.

The process
1. Examine the root causes and not just the symptoms because in this case, they could have doubled the telephone staff and not made much difference.
2. Set an objective.
3. Develop an action plan to address the root causes.
4. Implement and measure the results. Remember what I have said throughout this book - *measure everything you can!* You would be shocked at the number of companies who go into large projects and ignore the measurements.

The information to handle the customers' questions was not at hand. Simple questions like "Where is my order?" could not be answered. Further, the phone reps did not know what authority they had to help satisfy the customer and there was not a formal escalation procedure in place. Finally, there was not a load balancing process so they could not handle the peak volumes and changeovers.

The objective
Staff must be able to answer and close 95% of all customer calls within one minute!

The action plan
The key questions asked by customers were analyzed to minimize surprises. A procedure was laid out to resolve

each issue within the objective time frame. In some cases this required automation changes. A load balancing system was implemented, formal training was performed and delegated authority procedures including an escalation process, were put in place.

The results

Within 5 months, less people were handling more calls, wait times averaged under a minute and the drop out rate was 5%. The average call length was just over 1 minute, customer satisfaction was high and cancellations dropped significantly. Lastly, employee morale skyrocketed.

"Thank you for calling our Technical Support Hotline. The longest we've ever kept anyone on hold was 19 hours and 23 minutes. If you break that record today, you will win $10,000! Good luck!"

Financial management and reporting systems

Your financial management and reporting systems must meet the needs of various internal and external audiences.

These include you and your management team, investors both private and public, lenders and regulators.

To create a financial reporting system you need to start with a basic accounting system. Forget Excel except as an analysis tool. If you are large enough to support an in-house accounting group, they will already have chosen an accounting package. The preference of a package can be much more of a religious choice than a functional one. Just be sure that the chosen package can accommodate your expected growth.

If you are a small business that out sources your accounting but uses an accounting package to write cheques and record routine transactions, I would suggest a package like QuickBooks but there are many others that will work as well. You or your bookkeeper should enter the transaction records in house. This will give you immediate reporting on invoices, receivables and cash. Additionally, you will not be paying an accounting firm to do the basic entry and balancing. If you don't do this in house, your first bill will be a shock.

Many of the accounting packages contain 'canned' reports that you can use. Be sure to work with your accountant to define them. In spite of the fact that you might hate accounting as I do, learn to read the reports! Here are some examples of the reports that you might expect to get:
- Summary of Results - key information on one page
- Balance Sheet - include financial ratios
- Income Statement - profit and loss (P/L)
- Cash Flow Statement - can differ significantly from P/L
- Departmental P/L's - include key operating information and financial ratios

- Management Commentary and Analysis - needed for external investors.

Build a model and a budget. Most financial packages contain standard functions for this and enable you to forecast future performance and financing requirements. Manage your budget and hold your people accountable.

Cash flow statement
The cash flow statement is the critical report in your financial management system and it can differ significantly from the P/L statement. It includes the cost of new investments; timing of A/R collections and A/P payments but excludes items such as depreciation, deferred taxes, etc. The cash flow statement can be prepared on a daily, weekly or monthly basis depending on your business requirements.

You should also run comparison reports that compare P/L and cash flow for each:
- Month - actual vs. budget
- Year to Date - actual vs. budget/prior year
- Full Year Forecast - latest forecast vs. original budget/prior year.

Budget process
You need to begin early with guidelines built from bottom up and involve department managers to determine what they can control or influence. It should be month by month for each department and approved by senior management. A consolidated report is also required. It is key that you not

only measure everything you can but constantly compare outcomes against expectations.

The following checklist can be used to test your financial reporting requirements:
- Are reports produced on a timely basis?
- Are they understandable and not overwhelmed by detail?
- Can the system/model accommodate new departments?
- Can department heads be held accountable for their results?
- Are peak financing requirements known?
- Do you have good explanations of variances?
- Do your accounting/finance people have the necessary skills?
- Are there significant year-end adjustments by auditors?

I had an experience with one company that had $40 million dollars in errors against a $7 million dollar inventory! How does this happen? The company was essentially running with no controls whatsoever and when hard times hit, they were in deep, deep trouble.

REFERENCES

Enterprise-Wide Software Solutions:Integration Strategies and Practices by Sergio Lozinsky

Process Redesign: The Implementation Guide for Managers by Arthur R. Tenner and Irving J. DeToro.

ROADRUNNER TECHNOLOGIES

What Bob discovered as the orders came in was that his staff was not able to easily answer some of the customers basic questions. All the information was somewhere on the local area network, but contained in separate files and nothing was linked together. He decided to implement a resource planning system using an entry-level, but scalable package (e.g. Syspro) supported by a local consultant. This would take time to implement so his team wrote down all the key questions they needed to answer and set up a procedure manual that enabled staff to access the information quickly. The procedures manual was necessary to support the systems installation anyways and other procedures were addressed like sales forecasting and personnel management. Roadrunners' accounting systems were based on QuickBooks and produced the financial and cash statements he required to run the business. He upgraded to a new package better linked to the resource planning software. Things were going well and Bob needed to hire more staff. He also learned that some of his existing employees were not cutting it.

CHAPTER 6
Hire and manage people effectively

"If you pick the right people and give them the opportunity to spread their wings—and put compensation as a carrier behind it—you almost don't have to manage them."
Jack Welch

Failure symptoms:
- *Employee satisfaction is low*
- *Turnover is high*
- *Productivity is low but salary costs are high*
- *You are losing touch with the business.*

When starting out, often as a one-person business you might grow initially by bringing in family members. This has several advantages among which are reducing expenses and taxes. They're able to take on roles that require part time work and irregular hours (e.g. bookkeeping). However as you expand, they also bring some liabilities that need to be dealt with up front. For example, as the business grows you realize your sister's work-challenged son really should not have been hired in the first place. Family members are hard to fire without causing tension in the relationship. For example, do you lay off your wife or your best engineer? Lastly, relatives can misbehave because they believe have the inside track to the boss and are not subject to the same rules or consequences as other staff. Certain liberties, such as starting late, may be taken that cause resentment with the other staff members.

Remember that you are running a business to make a profit and while family is important they have to fit into the organization as it grows. It's important to know that 70% of family-run businesses don't make it to the 2nd generation and 90% don't make it to the 3rd. This failure rate is appalling so proceed with caution. There is plenty of excellent reading material in this area on the Internet.

Another good reference is *"Every Family's Business: A Blueprint for Protecting Family Business Wealth"*, by Thomas Deans.

Resumes

It's long been said that resumes are nothing more than marketing documents designed to tell employers what they want to hear. And given the talent shortages hitting many industries today, it's easy to see why hiring managers want to believe everything that they read. A resume is just the start of the hiring process, not the end. There is a lot of testing and checking that needs to be done. In fact, resumes and interviews are often not the primary determinants in a successful hire. Once you have identified similar skill levels, it has more to do with the with the culture of the organization and how the individual will fit in. You may be able to identify the fit yourself but both you and the prospective employee are in sell mode, so not all the filters may be working. There are psychological testing firms that can help you and while they might seem expensive, the cost of de-hiring is often many times more than the cost of hiring.

One of the benefits of today's environment is the availability of an older workforce. As baby boomers reach the age of retirement they become available to you as potential hires. These people tend to be highly educated and are backed by 20 or 30 years of experience. Many of them have underlying financial resources, are willing to take a chance and maybe not quite ready to retire yet. *(This was me when I left IBM.)* You may have to pay more than you would for lesser applicants, but depending on the candidate and your incentives, it will be significantly less than what they made during their recent career.

You may also have to be creative about how you package things such as options and profit sharing and vacations, but you should be able to come up with something attractive for the right candidate. In addition, many of them will be willing to work on contract for greater flexibility. The bottom line is you could access exceptional skills and experience for substantially less than a large company would have to pay.

One character to be wary of that I mentioned earlier is the one I call the *'Royal Smart Person'*. He or she might be responsible for taking your idea and implementing it with current technology. These characters can be paranoid, secretive and seemingly irreplaceable. But they also present a liability with missed schedules and convoluted designs geared to making them indispensable. I have come across the Royal Smart Person several times and often they get dangerously close to sinking the company before they are finally let go.

You need to have team players in your organization and you need to be the leader.

You will want to familiarize yourself with the labour laws in your area of business. In many jurisdictions stepping outside the boundaries may give you an employee for life. Consider using employment contracts even if you're not hiring contractors. They should specify the probationary period as well as other terms of employment. And if a mistake is made, act quickly to review the performance requirements and document it IN WRITING. If the desired improvement does not occur, fire them.

ROADRUNNER *or* ROADKILL

"I hate to terminate your employment, Mr. Kent, but we found traces of kryptonite in your urine."

Nobody likes the firing process, but it is a necessary function to be handled quickly and efficiently. In the end, it is actually easier on you and on the employee being terminated. In addition, if the process is properly documented you will be able to pay the minimum severance required by law. If you do not document it properly, you could be in for an expensive settlement where in most juristictions, the law leans towards the employee. I continue to be amazed at the number of companies I have worked with where inadequate employees are kept on the payroll for months and even years, after the problem has been identified.

When starting out in business you have to be the most knowledgeable, the best sales rep, the best accountant, the best engineer, the best lawyer, etc. But as your business grows and you add professional staff, the toughest thing for any new manager and particularly an entrepreneur have to deal with is delegation. When you have competent people you must be prepared to let them do the jobs that you hired them for. However, as your growth continues, be sure to use one of the most powerful management techniques for keeping in touch with your business... *Management By Walking Around (MBWA).* MBWA will continue to keep you grounded in reality, but it MUST be planned and scheduled. This is particularly true in this age of electronic media. Shutting yourself in your office with your email, spreadsheets and meetings on your turf will not keep you in touch with reality. Schedule at least 30 minutes several times a week to get out to look, listen and lead!

"Either lead, follow, or get out of the way.
But never try to do all three at the same time!"

One of the best books that I have found on leadership is *"Leadership Wisdom from the Monk Who Sold His Ferrari"* by Robin Sharma.

Checklist for hiring and managing people effectively
- Capitalize on the changing workforce
- Prepare for the perils of the family business. Have a plan that everyone understands
- The Royal Smart Person, closely manage indispensable people
- Delegate effectively.

ROADRUNNER TECHNOLOGIES

Fortunately, Bob had implemented a performance evaluation and documentation system right from the start, which was a result of his corporate discipline kicking in. As the business grew, he insisted (and monitored) all his managers ensure that performance reviews were up to date. So when the time came to cull the herd, they could do it with the minimum amount of pain. There were however, a couple of key technical skills that he needed to back up before he could make any other moves (remember indispensable people can be a liability). Reducing his personnel expenses helped him to shore up other areas. He also continued to monitor the company through MBWA, so that he had a close handle on the operations of the company and the staff felt empowered to continue doing the right things. In addition, he added some management strength by hiring a couple of over 50's like himself who were excited to be involved in a growing enterprise. One of these was a sales manager who brought in good discipline, but also presented some new challenges.

CHAPTER 7
Balance marketing and sales

"Drive thy business or it will drive thee."
Benjamin Franklin

"You can say the right thing about a product and nobody will listen. You've got to say it in such a way that people will feel it in their gut."
William Bernbach

Failure symptoms:
- *Low sales productivity*
- *Excessive marketing and sales expenses*
- *Inability to measure the above*
- *Unmotivated sales staff*
- *Confusing and inconsistent price structure*
- *Long-term goals sacrificed for short-term sales.*

Maximizing marketing effectiveness

Sales and marketing are two complementary but very different functions in any company. Their relative balance will depend on the company and its products. A simple way to look at it is:
- A company that has small value products sold to thousands of customers will be *marketing driven*
- A company that has high value products sold to a few well-defined customers will be a *sales driven*
- Both are *market driven.*

Sales is not the fast talking guys in loud suits; it is a process. Marketing is not a graphics/web designer or even an advertising manager; it is part of the same continuous process. If you are looking at the market through a telescope, you are a marketer. If you are looking at the market through a magnifying glass, you are a salesman.

Why is marketing so important today? People are bombarded with over 3,000 marketing messages daily! If that number seems high, go to the store, fast-forward through your recorded TV programs or drive to work. The messaging is termed 'clutter'. So how do you stand out? On average, search engines index over 100 million pages and your website is often first real exposure for your clients, even if you have a sales force. Think about how many times you have searched the web for information on a company before you speak to them. This means that the positioning of your product, service and company, are vital to your survival. Marketing should be viewed as the key to earning permission for continued and meaningful dialogue ultimately resulting in sales.

There are tools and techniques to ensure your website is found in searches. For example, the more links you have to other sites, the higher the probability your site will be found. For this you need to talk to your web designer or programmer and make sure he or she can deliver this for you.

Have objectives and measurements for everything

I am constantly surprised by the number of companies who spend money on marketing without having an objective or a means of measuring the effectiveness of the marketing tool. The reasons can include things like "We have to do it because our competitors are doing it." Maybe the competitor knows something and maybe they don't. They may have different objectives from you. Whether it's a trade show, an ad, or a website, be sure to ask the tough questions:
- Why are we doing this?
- What is our objective?
- How do we measure success?
- Is it sustainable?
- Is it consistent with our positioning?

Now ask the same questions of your competitors' efforts. You may learn how to better compete with them and also learn more about yourself. *(For an outline of a Marketing Plan please see the Appendix.)*

> *"Know yourself and know your enemy and you will win a thousand battles."*
> **Basic Sun Tzu**

EXAMPLES

Here are a couple of examples of the lack of measurements hiding major mistakes:

1. A Direct Response company I was contracted with had placed a series of ads and to quote the marketing manager, "We got a heck of a deal". When I asked to see the tracking information, he said the sales reps were too busy to record them. This was unacceptable so we instituted a system for tracking the ads and when analysed, he found out his $50,000 deal had resulted in less than $4,000 in sales. Needless to say, the ad was dropped and the tracking system was strictly enforced in future campaigns.

2. When I asked to see tracking data on another company's website, they were quite proud of the number of hits they were getting. What emerged was the site was good in that a lot of people found it, but was so poorly designed that people quickly left. What was worse, they had no tracking mechanism to find out who they were so they could not do any follow-up on the contacts. The site needed significant changes. Remember, every

marketing communication is a conversation with the customer leading to an ultimate sale. It is imperative that you track the conversation.

Remember the 4 P's for a marketing plan

When IBM was the industry leader in PC Sales, we constantly scanned the competitors' ads, trade press rumours, personnel changes and any other info we could get our hands on. We tracked sales - theirs and ours. We developed strategy packages that mimicked the competitors' positioning and then decided on our marketing strategy - pre-emptive or reactive. This section covers the strategy portion of the marketing plan, but before you get there, you need to understand your marketing mix, which starts with the 4 P's.

But before we discuss the 4 P's, I will let you in on the 4 greatest secrets of successful marketing:
- Rule 1 - Be first!
- Rule 2 - If you can't be first, find something to be first in!
- Rule 3 - Perception is everything, what your potential customers think of you is reality!
- Rule 4 - Measure everything. If you can't measure it, don't do it!

The four P's are: *Product, Price, Place* and *Promotion*. More time will be spent on price in this section because it is probably the most neglected of the P's. It is also the area where the most money is left on the table. Sufficient time will also be spent on Promotion as it is constantly changing.

Product

Product (or service) is not really a "thing" in marketing terms. It is a positioning and value statement. It is something that solves a client's problem, saves them money or has some other intrinsic value. The Product needs to be consistently aligned with the company's positioning and add value to the Brand. It cannot diminish the Brand unless there is a desire to change the positioning.

When IBM launched its' PC, it created a new positioning distancing itself from the stuffy corporate image while at the same time, enhancing the IBM Brand. The product's attributes appealed to the early adopters in a fledgling industry and took risks on little known companies like Microsoft and Intel. The key value that really sold the IBM PC was the openness of the software and hardware interfaces that allowed many companies to build applications that further enhanced the PC's value. It was simply positioned for anyone and everyone with an abundance of value added software to make life easier. This is the reasoning behind the image of a single rose for simplicity and the little tramp character representing the common man in the ad campaigns that ran from 1982-1984.

In short, a product is definable and succinct. It has a clear, understandable and unique positioning. It adds value and is defined by the client in terms of needs satisfied and value provided, not in its' technical specs or offering descriptions. If you want an example of a highly technical product that was marketed successfully, look no further than the Sony® Walkman or more recently, the Apple® iPod.

Price

Price is often the most neglected component of the marketing science. Often people use cost plus because they haven't fully thought through their strategy. A price communicates many things such as quality and value, and must be consistent with your positioning and objectives.

To come up with a pricing strategy, start with a set of assumptions about your company and the market for a 12-month period. If you get your pricing assumptions right, the pricing strategy and rest of the marketing plan will fall into place. If the assumptions change, the plan is easily modified. Price communicates many messages so it must make sense over time. Set out assumptions on a time scale. These include:
- Your product plan
- Value to customer, which may evolve over time
- Competitive plan (assumptions). These can be found in the trade press, Internet, surveys, advertising and even investigative services who will do a competitive profile for a fee. You often meet your competition at trade shows or business meetings. Be sure to ask lots of questions and you will be amazed at how you can profile companies in your industry.
- Barriers to entry such as patents, licenses, and skill requirements, scale of operations needed to hit cost points.

Pick a methodology or methodologies, consistent with your positioning, market maturity, customer value and timing assumptions. Write it down and monitor it constantly! Here are just a few of the methodologies you can choose from:

- *Price leader* - A price leader anticipates the market and is the first out with the best price.
- *Price follower* - A price follower follows the market, but has a plan with what they will do if the market changes. For example, we will always meet competition.
- *Price skimming* - A price skimmer gets the maximum profit from a product while they have a new exclusive. A good example of this is Sony, who is never the cheapest but constantly innovates to command a price premium. Sony also has a white label brand (Akai) to compete in the commodity market.
- *Value price* - A value priced strategy is not necessarily the cheapest but is perceived as the best price or value based on the customers' needs, definition of quality or simple but adequate product features. A value price strategy may lead to a higher priced product because of a large amount of perceived value to the customer. *(This is similar to limit pricing).*
- *Premium price* - A premium priced product is perceived as the leader in both quality and features to demand a higher price. A premium price strategy may also be a skimming strategy depending on the product and the market. Skimming depends on high product feature turnover.
- *Limit price* - Limit pricing depends on a good understanding of customer value and pricing to what the market will bear. This is generally employed when there are barriers to entry and limits on production. For example, if you have an exclusive product but can only make 10 units a year, charge as much as your customers are will-

ing to pay. This is also popular with consultants where there is an exclusive skill, reputation or personality that can demand a premium price (e.g. Bill Clinton or Tom Peters). A word of caution, if you price too low with a limited ability to deliver, you risk alienating customers due to too many unfulfilled orders.
- *Bundled vs. unbundled* - Bundled pricing tends to include other items in the price charged. For example, service or support, free upgrades or follow-on examinations to be bundled into the price. Unless a company is recognized as being superior in these elements, this can be dangerous if the competition is unbundled. In addition, many companies make more profit on the after sales service than they do on the primary offerings. For years car dealerships made little or no money on selling cars, but good profits on service and accessories. Some promotional bundles can have short-term value that change or expand the target. (e.g. special software, free gas for a year, etc.)
- *Cost plus* - Cost plus is a valid methodology and is generally based on what is needed to cover expenses plus a mark up for the company. It is common in commodity industries and when companies don't know anything else. Another caution, don't do it unless you have a good read on all your market assumptions to measure your price against.

"When your price is very high, people assume that your product must be very good!"

In summary:
- Price communicates messages
- Prices are not static
- A pricing strategy is one of the most fundamental activities so write it down
- Monitor the assumptions constantly.

EXAMPLE

The Can Company is purely fictitious but is based on real products and experiences although somewhat simplified. Think back to when metal soft drink cans first came on the market. The Can Company manufactures these cans and is viewed as high service and an industry innovator enabling them to price 10-15% above the competition.

Their unique value proposition is that they are the first to offer painted labels rather than paper, which made it possible for them to skim prices for six months. As a result of their volume, they are the low cost manufacturer and have several patents on the current product, which will soon expire. As innovators, they have developed a new pull-tab that will be available in six months and an improved version that will come out in 12. Based on trade press and customer comments, the competition is rumored to have an equivalent tab coming out at a lower price in 6 months and another with better technology in 12 months.

The Can Company's strategy is to preempt the competition with a price drop and introduce the new pull-tab at a price slightly higher than the current product doing the same with the improved easy to open product later on. Shown graphically you can see that the strategy could maximize revenue and keep the competition at bay, while preserving the company's high quality and innovative positioning. However, this depends on the competition. As they say in military terms, "No plan lasts beyond the first contact with the enemy so be prepared to change." If the competition fails in the timing, the Can Company may choose to hold off on the price reduction and skim price the new products. There are many more scenarios, but the important point is to have a plan and not just react to the competition.

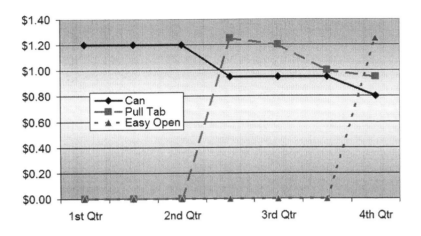

Place

There are many ways to get your product to the end user including direct and telephone sales, resellers, distributors, web sales and agents. A service example of this has been laser eye surgery where companies have paid optometrists to direct business their way. Ideally you will have many of these channels. If they do include direct sales remember, it is just another channel and you will want to avoid or minimize unnecessary channel conflict.

The key to successful channel management is ensuring that there is something in it for everyone. When you make money, the channel partners make money. Be sure that your margins make sense over time as many markets in high volume products get commoditized the intermediary inevitably gets squeezed.

To select your channels successfully you have to look at where and how your customers buy products like yours. This will vary from country to country. Then look at likely channel partner candidates. Be careful because some will overlap and some will appear to overlap but in reality may be focused on different market segments. When you choose a partner, remember this is a long-term relationship so both parties must be committed to the relationship. Set sales targets *(hard or soft)* and measurements in your agreement, then monitor and meet often to review.

It is key to train the channels' staff and put in place a promotional plan. Remember that channels are not sellers but rather order takers. Picture yourself going into a computer store to buy a laptop. If you say you want a laptop, then the floor rep will present you with 5 or 6 and test your budget. If you say you want an HP, the conversation is very different. You as the marketer must set the precedent.

A word of caution, channels can be very hard and expensive to get rid of. This is particularly true of sales agents in foreign countries where they get agreements from several companies. Despite your strategy or product features, they will always go after the low hanging fruit. When you try to disengage, you may be in for a long battle.

For example I once contracted with a Taiwanese agent who couldn't possibly deliver, but who was well connected in the country. If we cut him, Taiwan sales could stop all together out of loyalty to him. It took an expensive year to negotiate out of the agent agreement. The process was long and required very delicate handling. Our company ended up hiring a very experienced Taiwanese sales representative, which resulted in significantly more sales to the Taiwanese manufacturers.

Web based sales *(e.g. Direct Response)* are again another channel. They are much more dependent on promotion than channel management. In most cases, you will hire an outside *(often offshore)* firm to manage the order fulfillment. Today it is often too expensive and unnecessary to have an in-house fulfillment organization. The bottom line on Place is you have lots of choices. Pick the ones that best match your customers, train them and promote the product or service yourself.

Promotion

Promotion is the art of getting your message across to your customer in an increasingly cluttered media environment. The final objective is having the privilege of selling something to that customer. We know that the average North American is bombarded with roughly 3,000 thousand advertising related messages daily. To have any hope of measurable affect, your communication must speak to your customer clearly, concisely with a consistent look and feel familiar to them and their influencers. It must always reinforce their perceptions of everything to do with you and your company's positioning. To that end, every communication must have:
- An objective
- A call to action
- A measurement system.

Remember, you're not in the business of winning creative awards; you are there to accomplish a goal so evaluate everything against these three tests. Ads that have great stopping power may not cause people to take action or even remember your product or service. Be very critical of any creative that looks nice but doesn't accomplish your goals. In addition, you are not necessarily representative of your audience so you personally liking an ad may not be important. Always put yourself in your customers' shoes.

One example of this was in the early days of PC marketing at IBM, the president phoned to say he didn't like an ad. I pointed out to him that when we target CEO's of large companies, he would be a good test. Then I explained what we were trying to accomplish and explained that it is not a matter of *liking something*; it is about accomplishing a goal.

Another example takes me to my winter home in Panama. There is an ad on the airport expressway that features a strikingly beautiful woman. I always noticed it but didn't know what it was for until a friend asked, "What kind of watch is she selling"? For the next few visits I tried to find out and to this day I still do not know what the brand was or who was selling them. It had great stopping power, but definitely an unfulfilled objective.

When spending your promotion budget, remember that frequency will trump reach every time. For example, one ad on the Super Bowl may reach millions but seven well-placed communications to a targeted/qualified audience will get results. This is what we call the '7X Principle'. On average, humans retain about 14% of what they see or hear at any time so to get 100% of your message across you need to get it to them 7 times. Frequency always trumps reach. Always.

Remember to address every stakeholder in your communications. Often your employee, shareholders, suppliers and other stakeholders can be important audiences to service.

Marketing should be treated as business management and planning, not graphic art. Demand ROI for each marketing dollar. Bottom line - there are ways to measure effectiveness so *if you can't measure it, don't do it*!

Normally, marketing should not report to sales, but should be responsible for sales effectiveness! Marketing and sales are two different but complementary functions. And often when things are going well, each department will take credit and when sales are off target, they can be quick to point a finger in an almost adversarial battle for budget. Like research and development, marketing focuses on the long term and sales the short term. Make sure you have a manager who is accountable for measurable objectives.

Forget the Internet and your website at your peril.

Not only is the message environment jam packed, we are all virtually connected. High-speed cable, wireless mobile, office and home computing search-connected devices are now only conspicuous when not in evidence. At the very least, assume that you and your suppliers, customers, competitors, funders, bankers and influencers are one big family sitting in the same room. Promotionally speaking, the Internet and your website are powerful tools for sales when properly deployed - more now than ever before.

Internet promotional tools include a number of web applications that are interactive, informative, user-centered and collaborative. Termed *Web 2.0* in 2004, these promotional modalities include web-based communities, hosting services, web applications, social networking, video-sharing sites, wikis, blogs, mashups and the like. These are widely used in what is termed *'engagement styles of marketing'* as practiced in social media communications.

With engagement styles of marketing you have the ability to use the power of the web to go far beyond traditional broadcast media. In fact, you can establish direct dialog with targeted customers and prospects by using applications like YouTube™, Twitter™, Facebook®, MySpace™, Second Life® and LinkedIn®, to promote your brand.

Common online techniques include optimizing press release content and making them click-interactive, search engine optimization (SEO), promoting social book-marking links, share widgets and cyber tagging your releases on Web 2.0 social tagging sites.

Some executives have a lot to say relevant to their field so you may need to develop a blog strategy. Interactive online pressrooms, link media *(old and new)* to recent and archived press releases. Company logos in various formats, photos and fact sheets, bios of your executive and management team members, along with contact information are the norm and are important parts of promotion.

According to Marketing Sherpa's business technology marketing benchmark guide www.marketingsherpa.com, 78% of technology buyers say they have listened to more than one technology-related podcast. There are an increasing number of podcast production and promotion tools available. Producing podcasts and webinars are an excellent way to share thought-leadership content online. There are many web conferencing services available that will fit your needs and budget.

These all share a common technical thread called viral marketing. Simply put, it is word of mouth in a much more effective form (e.g. Skype™ and YouTube). Viral marketing describes any strategy that encourages individuals to pass on a marketing message to others, creating the potential for exponential growth in the message's exposure and influence. Like viruses, such strategies take advantage of rapid multiplication to explode the message from thousands to millions. Viral marketing depends on effective testing of your websites ability to create links. It is best to involve a specialist and will be worth the investment. A good introductory link is http://www.wilsonweb.com/wmt5/viral-principles.htm.

Internet promotional tactics should convert lookers into buyers. Messaging and using targeted interactive marketing content strategies will increase website traffic and grow your customer groups. These promotional tactics can and should be organized and measured.

FURTHER READING

One of the most recognizable and successful deployments of all current styles of promotion has to be the story of President Obama's recent presidential campaign. The details can be found in a great article from marketingmag.com. by Matt Granfield. I encourage you to go online and read about it at http://www.publicrelationssydney.com.au/2009/how-social-media-won-obama-the-us-election.

CASE STUDY

The Stop Dump Site 41 Coalition protest north of Toronto in Tiny Township engaged MRC Partners (http://mrcpartners.wordpress.com) to promote their cause. The campaign is a good example of using a variety of media and social networking tools. It achieved a 1-year moratorium on August 25, 2009.

It began with organizing and establishing media contacts and created more than 100 direct to journalist in box press releases in a 4.5-month period. MRC distributed information, media materials and ongoing news updates to most related media in Canada and in the US via the American Water Trust. This created a great deal of media coverage - print, radio, TV and Web (http://stopdumpsite41.ca) in a short time and used social media, specifically the Twitter site at (http://twitter.com/StopDumpSite41).

An overview of coverage

Coverage on the CBC, TVO and CTV TV Networks and talk radio achieved approximately 100 mentions. Google had 6,270 hits on a "Dump Site 41", search and the website had 38,000 hits in Aug 09 including some by the US government. The twitter site covered this topic developed 348 followers (many were media producers).

A total of 25 stories appeared in the 3 major newspapers and local papers had printed 100 stories.

Important Note: You can see from the above that MRC Partners paid attention to measurement.

The results

Public perception of the issues grew rapidly. The DS41 protest became a cause celebrated and endorsed by more than 20 large associations/foundations. Recently, the County retained the services of high focus PR firm for a projected fee of $ 250,000 while MRC accomplished incredible results pro bono. The Simcoe County Council voted to close the dump and stopped any future development.

Point of interest

Accountants are using social media to connect with clients and other organizations. At Stambaugh Ness, LinkedIn provides a way to monitor the pulse of the business environment, while specialized networking software allows employees to respond to customer needs. *"There is urgency to these communications, and we'd better be willing to step up if we want to be competitive,"* said company President, Steve Hake.

In summary, begin with a plan, set measurable objectives, test and monitor continually, provide perceived value with every communication and forget the web at your peril.

MRC Partners (http://mrcpartners.wordpress.com/) is a Toronto-based market intelligence, PR and business development group that helps commercialize start-ups and early stage small caps. MRC has run several successful campaigns using the new media and social networking vehicles.

Managing a sales team

As indicated earlier, sales are a process and a key part of the process is how you reward and manage the sales team. Often mistakes are made for reasons, which on the surface sound reasonable. For example, many people don't think the salesmen should make more than the engineers. This would be fair if the engineers risked 30% or more of their salary if things didn't work out *(see risk and quota setting below)*, but most won't and so there has to be a premium for that risk. If the sales representative delivers 100% of target they usually receive a 10-20 % bonus.

A good sales representative is a different sort of person. He or she thrives on risk wanting a chance to hit it big with 150% of his or her target being a typical goal. They usually like high leverage plans that will deliver the opportunity. They measure themselves by the achievement, which is counted in dollars. By contrast most engineers measure success through peer recognition. Here are some guidelines for getting the most out of your sales team:

1. Set a high leverage plan that rewards overachievement. I am not in favor of a sales plan where the base is over 60% and ideally it's 50% or less. There are many industries where the sales teams are purely on commission. You can give a draw of 70 or 80% of the 100% target to make sure that they can feed their families, but no more. When long product sell cycles are involved, you will have to modify this principal for the first year.

    I will never forget my first sales cheque from IBM, which was not only 20% lower than the salary cheque, but it had a note at the bottom that stated the amount

I had been loaned by IBM for the draw. My automatic reaction was to say *"I better get out there and sell something"*.
2. Set a plan that focuses on what you want to sell and make sure that you set the quota objectives aggressive but fair. You can easily reduce them for unforeseen market conditions, but be cautious about raising them part way through a quota year. Remember, that when you set the plan, you are telling the sales team what to sell so if they blow the doors off the plan, celebrate it, don't criticize it. If they sell the wrong things, it is you that set the plan and if someone makes more money in a year than the president, rejoice... their value and yours' has just increased.

   The quota and the plan is a contract between you and your sales team. It has a finite period, usually a year (but could be quarterly or semi-annually renewed). When you change the terms mid contract, it should be considered a negotiation, not an edit.
3. Remember when getting input for quota setting that all sales people sandbag and the best ones are masters at it. Be sure to take it as one piece of input *(see the forecasting section)*. Usually if nobody says they are happy, you have a realistic plan.
4. Also know that sales people will always go for the low hanging fruit first in spite of your sales plan, so you might have to divide territories or product lines appropriately. When focusing on new business, which is the lifeblood of the company, successes are often slower and harder to get but the new business sales person should have

similar leverage opportunities to one who focuses on milking the existing accounts.

"Our old mission statement was more eloquent, and dignified, but not nearly as effective."

ROADRUNNER TECHNOLOGIES

The new sales manager that Bob hired was used to a disciplined forecasting system that would allow more accurate planning of inventory, resources and manufacturing requirements. He implemented this system along with a change to the sales incentive plan that provided more leverage to the sales people. (As a growing company, the original sales plan had a higher base salary with bonuses to deal with the longer sell cycles, but now the plan needed to incentivize revenue growth). Bob continued to have marketing report to him and not the sales manager so that he continued to control that strategic direction and maintain the positioning of the company and the products. Where they butted heads was often over pricing. The sales manager wanted a lower price, but Bob felt that the premium price for premium service was still where the positioning should be. They compromised by unbundling service and managing it as a business in itself. Soon, with professional service management, service contracts rapidly became a major contributor to profitability. All was going great guns and Bob began to relax, but storm clouds were brewing.

CHAPTER 8
When trouble emerges

*"Everyone has a plan –
until they get punched in the face."*
Mike Tyson

*"You can always amend a big plan, but
you can never expand a little one.
I don't believe in little plans. I believe in plans
big enough to meet a situation,
which we can't possibly foresee now."*
Harry S. Truman

Now comes the reality check. Trouble is inevitable in any business, so plan for it. Whether it is the economy, the industry, the competition or internal issues, how you react to it will ultimately define the difference between success and failure. The first rule is to look for the signs of trouble and act decisively. You have to get to the core problem and take targeted action. There are two things I have found that tell the tale of a business headed for failure. I have seen two fairly large businesses die as a result of:
1. Assuming they could sell themselves out of trouble
2. Cutting expenses by 10% across the board

Why these 'solutions' are ineffective is because they don't target the real problem. You need to identify what the problem is and equally important, what it is not. For example, what if sales are down because the market is finite, the competition has new products, the economy is bad and/or your cost structure is uncompetitive? You may be better off reducing costs and selling at the same level while developing new products or services. You need to understand why more people aren't buying rather than just raising quotas. In the end, it may be that the market is there and your sales force has become complacent and needs new 'challenges'.

So what is the secret of survival in troubled times? It comes down to three things:
1. *Leadership*: It is crucial to have someone at the helm that will make the tough decisions and make them quickly. Too often the environment is permeated by committees and meetings that dissolve into "woe is me" and non-action. The leader must listen to all the input, quickly

assess the highest leverage solutions and force action. For most of my business career, I had a brass sign on my desk that read, *"Let's find at least one reason why it can be done!"*

2. *Decisiveness:* Once a course of action is agreed to, act and act quickly. A former boss of mine used to joke, *"In the absence of any other plan, do something!"* In today's tough environment it seems less like a joke and more like a necessary call to action.

3. *Realism:* Like the company that says we will just sell more, many companies and leaders default to what appears to be a less painful course of action simply out of wishful thinking. When the swine flu hit Mexico, no amount of promotion or pricing was going to stave off disaster. In the short-term, hotels had to close and consolidate to cut losses. If your customers' industry is in a slump, selling them more is not an option. And, if you get bridge funding, don't put off the tough decisions *(like cutbacks and controls)* to follow an unrealistic plan. This is high time for another reality check!

Before you do anything else, recall Rule #1 – Cash is king! Remember GM and Chrysler of 2009? Enough said. You must do everything possible to ensure your cash from operations is preserved and that any marginal assets or expenses are sold or eliminated. This may include inventories, buildings and even the presidents Ferrari! Rethink your growth plans in terms of cash effectiveness. If the new venture or product is a cash drain, which is not underwritten by another funding vehicle, curtail or shelve it. Some of this may be counterintuitive, but you may find that while increasing prices reduces volume and growth, you may generate more cash.

Start by making a list of what the problems are and what they are not. Once this is on paper it will seem much more manageable. The first key is to remember your core business before you start of on a whole new tack. It is what got you to where you are and you may need to get back to basics. Many spectacular failures such as Circuit City and Ames have resulted from pursuit of new ventures at the expense of the core business. If Circuit City put the effort into their core business, their growth would have doubled and they still might be around today to duke it out with Best Buy! Before you leap, examine the core and what needs to be done to keep it profitable and growing.

A personal example comes from when I was on the board of a company called Taiwan Connection. Their core business was facilitating contract manufacturing for electronics companies. They wanted to see how they could switch their business to a new and more exciting area, but they didn't want to take on more staff to do it. Their solution was to get themselves away from their single largest customer. I objected as that customer was almost 25% of their business, paid their bills and continued to sole source through the Taiwan Connection. They complained but agreed temporarily. Not long after they blew their brains out on the new venture and unfortunately, had to sell out, not because the core was a problem, but because they could not sustain the failed new venture.

The second key area of failing is to forget your customer. This is very common with larger companies when they start to believe they know more than the customer. A perfect example of this was Motorola, who in the early days of the cell phone market 'owned' a more than 50% market share. They tried to use their muscle to force the cell phone providers to take their analog technology when the end users were asking for digital. The rebellion that followed left Motorola with less than 15% market share. Remember that not only is the customer right and their perceptions are your reality, but it is your privilege and not your right, to sell them something.

When you need to cut costs, do not do it across the board. This approach penalizes some areas more than others. It may be that instead of cutting the expenses of the Topeka office staffed by your wife's brother, that it should be closed outright and the resources be put into another more productive office.

To examine the areas where expense cutting is needed, you should employ benchmarking techniques. There is an abundance of information available about ratios for companies similar to your own. Some will come from publicly traded companies and industry groups, some from your knowledge of your competitors and possibly even from your accountant. Ask the hard questions about why your expense to revenue ratio is higher than similar companies, why are your turns lower, and why is your revenue per headcount so much lower? After you finish your list of these questions, you will have a much better idea of where to make cuts.

Nobody likes to fire or layoff people and it is one of the more stressful things you will have to do. One thing many managers do badly is deal with poor performance. Before you get to a layoff, make sure that your managers are dealing effectively with poor performance as a normal process. In order to fire someone you should have a performance appraisal system and for poor performers, a performance improvement program (PIP). If you institute a PIP on someone, make sure it is documented and accepted in writing.

About a third of the people you PIP will become satisfactory employees, about a third will quit and the last third you will have to fire, but it should be easy if you document it properly. This will ensure that you don't have much deadwood around when belt tightening is needed and will make you more cost competitive. Take a page from GE CEO Jack Welch, who raised the standard by 5% every year. If you are thinking about outsourcing, it can be effective, but remember that except for a few examples, outsourcing takes some time to pay back and you had better have the cash reserves to weather the transition.

When it comes to expense cutting the biggest area will be staff. As you grow, so does your staff, but when trouble comes make sure you and your managers have lifeboat lists of key employees so that cuts can be made intelligently. Pick your people, have HR set a process in place for exiting, check applicable labour laws, then act quickly and cut deep. By doing what the Chinese refer to as *'death by 1,000 cuts'*, you will sap your company's morale. When it is over, address the remaining employees to explain the situation, reassure them about the future and ask for their support in these tough times. If you execute this well and truthfully, you will probably find that remaining employees will work doubly hard to make the company successful under your new short-term plan.

Note: Here is one of the perils of a family business. Your top survival picks may not be (and usually are not) on your lifeboat list.

"We're willing to do whatever it takes to turn this company around, as long as you don't ask us do anything different."

CASE STUDIES

Before the major restructuring that led IBM on a new path, the common practice was to cut expenses by 10% across the board and leave departments to implement as they saw fit. In the PC Group, which was growing in sales, we had 4 administrative assistants for a staff of close to 100, after the cuts were made. In another department with flat sales and a staff of 30, they too had 4 administrative assistants who were often unoccupied and reading novels. Clearly, across the board cuts did not solve the problem, but did create many meetings to justify various provincial positions. When IBM did their major restructuring from 1994-1996, they did it with a strategic direction in place and as a result, emerged as a much stronger company.

At one point, a company called Sidus Systems had more branch offices in Canada than IBM for one-tenth the sales. They needed to close many of them, but ran into family employment issues. Their solution was across the board cuts. Additionally, when asked how they would solve their problem, the president replied, "We'll sell more". What they needed was a strategy to implement a survival plan and without it, Sidus ceased to exist.

At another company called Image Processing, we had over 100 people working for us when the economic downturn occurred in 1999. We needed to preserve cash flow in order to position for the next opportunities for growth. Reducing travel costs and other quick solutions had already been implemented. We first laid out our strategic imperatives and then made 2 lists. The first was of the key employees needed to achieve our goals and the other the rating lifeboat list by department. Every senior executive got to vote and then the majority decision was adhered to. We put the lowest ranked employees on the layoff list and other, key employees on a transfer list as required. We took deep cuts in numbers so that we would not have to come back in a month to do more, which would cause creeping morale problems.

We also froze executive bonuses and cut some senior managers. The Human Resources and legal staffs were consulted to put together fair packages and avoid labour issues. We then acted quickly and announced it to the staff with as full disclosure as possible, of the strategic reasons for the action. Not only did the staff accept the actions, we found out afterwards that they knew some of the people who were let go were not pulling their weight. Image Processing continued to grow and was eventually acquired by Photon Dynamics.

"At one point, I had seventeen vice presidents. That's when I realized it was time to restructure the company and get back to basics."

There are many other crises that need to be dealt with quickly. For example, if your capital dries up you need a cash management system like the one discussed in Chapter 4. If it is competitive pressure, make sure you plan for it and watch for the signals. If you run into problems with the press, don't avoid them, take them head on and you will defuse them quicker than you think.

Bottom line, act quickly and decisively and you have a good chance of weathering the storm.

An excellent reference for more ideas on crisis management is: "*Leadership in the Era of Economic Uncertainty*" by Ram Charan.

ROADRUNNER TECHNOLOGIES

Bob's company had grown rapidly and a few stress cracks were starting to show. When the economic downturn hit, the basic infrastructure was in place enabling them to weather the storm. While they were pursuing new product lines, Bob made sure that they kept the eye on the core business and it continued to grow until his customers started to cut back. When the storm clouds started to form they sat down and quickly revised their plans. Bob had instituted a major cost cutting program that allowed him to sell a differentiated lower cost product with some new service offerings that not only met some of his customers needs for lower cost, but also surprised his competitors. Because of MBWA, Bob and his managers kept in close touch with the workers. They did one round of layoffs and froze executive bonuses. When Bob announced it to the staff he gave them full disclosure on the plans to keep the company profitable. Bob's company not only weathered the storm, but because of the slow reaction from some of his competitors he actually grew revenue and continued to be profitable. As the economic crisis cleared Roadrunner Technologies was already planning for their future growth.

CHAPTER 9
Checklist for the future

"Have a plan. Follow the plan, and you'll be surprised how successful you can be. Most people don't have a plan. That's why it's easy to beat most folks."
Paul "Bear" Bryant, Football Coach
University of Alabama's Crimson Tide

"Planning is bringing the future into the present so that you can do something about it now."
Alan Lakein

"Good fortune is what happens when opportunity meets with planning."
Thomas Alva Edison

In this final chapter, I have chosen to give you checklists of things to keep an eye on and help you grow your business in the future. They all relate back to the topics in the previous chapters but focus more on the future rather than the current essentials.

Think scale – "build to the vision"
Assess every move in terms of where your company will be, not where it is. It has been stressed by many of the gurus in business, the importance of vision. Take a practical approach to vision because becoming another Google or Microsoft takes a lot more than vision. I can tell you that when I met Bill Gates in the early days, he did not envision the mega company Microsoft is today. However, he surrounded himself with good people and built his company on a vision that would build a standard operating system for most PC's.

Build your systems, processes, products, services with this same open-ended vision, so that if you hit a long ball, you can capitalize on it without hiccups. Always ask, "Can we scale this quickly and profitably?"

Monitor your key indicators – what's critical?
Many businesses go into planning cycles that focus on revenue and profit targets. Jack Rockhart developed a methodology called "Critical Success Factors" which focuses on what you need to absolutely get right to survive and prosper. A practical implementation is found in Jan King's book "Business Plans to Game Plans: A Practical Guide for Turning Strategies into Actions". These factors vary by business and

time but include things like; cash flow, receivables, expense management, development costs, time to customer *(meeting promises),* marketing effectiveness *(finding new customers)* and customer satisfaction. Realistically, you can only manage 3 to 5 of these as a business manager. Accessing 'real time' data that measures your key indicators is critical. Don't get carried away with analysis, but don't overlook its benefits either. Share the information with your team for the most impact.

Keep your eye on the "core"

You need to clearly know where you are going, and what will get you there. Keep focused on your core business and avoid seemingly profitable side trips that take away from your positioning, core skills and business focus. One business I was associated with needed to acquire a company to get more capital. Unfortunately, it was not our core business and it took away significant management focus. A year later, we were in a cash crunch and I spent several "happy" months in Chicago trying to divest ourselves of the company.

Money is a "full-time job"

An internal or external expert is critical to finding 'adequate' cash through every channel and monitoring its' use. Forecast for the best and worst case scenarios to target your cash needs. Share the numbers with those who need them, who are responsible for them and hold them accountable. Have a system that shows the variances and more importantly, explain and learn from the variances. Remember, no matter what your business is… *cash is king!*

People

People come in two flavours - customers and staff/partners. Study the demographic trends and prepare for changes as they occur because one or more will affect your business. For example, in the middle of a recession you can have your pick of staff. However, this will change and so you need a strategy to retain not only your investment in employees and customers, but also for stakeholders such as main channels, key suppliers and bankers. Make sure you constantly evaluate performance, not just when the cash crunch hits. Consider outsourcing what others do better. It is often cheaper in the long run and much easier to scale. But do this carefully as you still need to retain control.

Act quickly/Just do it/Tomorrow it happens faster

Change is occurring at a very rapid rate. Technology is constantly increasing communication so be sure to focus on what improves your business. You can always learn a lot more about your competitors and your competitors will know more about you.

After reading this book you can plan for trouble and be ready to act as decisively and quickly as you would when taking advantage of new opportunities.

The web is taking over

Think about the number of times you access the Internet in a day. Prepare to work via the Internet and understand its potential. Your presence on the web will be the key introduction for your company if it isn't already. But ensure Internet use is focused on company needs. It is not a creative tool. It is a communications and goal-achieving tool! Neat graphics may take away from your goal and don't forget the *'3 clicks and you're gone'* rule.

Stay externally focused

Don't get caught up with *your* needs. If you can't fulfill your customers' needs, yours don't even matter. Be aware of what's happening to your markets, customers, competitors and suppliers.

Get to the customer effectively – 'Stay linked and learn'

Who and how can you best access the customer? Often your best relationship is not directly with the customer but through a channel, which includes the Internet. Understand how your channels work and why, and know where the customer relationship stands so you can continually reinforce it.

Set your practical goals and expectations

If you have an objective for return on investment *(and you should for all investments),* what is everyone's role - employees, suppliers, channels, partners, etc.? Do you know? Do they?

CHECKLIST FOR THE FUTURE

"It makes no sense to worry about the future. By the time you get there, it's the past!"

Closing thoughts

With your eye on the future first plan to address your current essentials and always keep these in mind as you build your business:

- Start with a good idea and test it
- Get your positioning right
- Get your funding in line
- Manage cash and expenses like they are your own
- Build processes and systems for where you want to be
- Hire and manage your people effectively
- Balance marketing and sales, and measure everything
- Look for the signs of trouble and act

… and never forget your customers!

As I said at the beginning, this book cannot guarantee you success. Fortunately, most managers do not make all of the errors we have discussed, but if you have picked up just one or two business saving ideas from this, then the effort was worth it. I wish you luck and prosperity.

David Morrison

Visit My Blog: http://roadrunnerorroadkill.typepad.com/

APPENDIX
Business Plan Outline

Below is an outline of topics you will need to effectively produce a business plan. There are many options available online and your investment banker may also have a template so check it out before using this one. The form should be narrative when it is developed and you will need a bulleted presentation as well. I have written a number of business plans and the best one are usually comprehensive but succinct.

There are two important reasons for doing a business plan. The first will be that you require one to get any funding. However, a more important reason is that you need to ask yourself all of the questions posed to effectively think through the viability and success criteria of your business. The two most important sections of your business plan are the Executive Summary, which should be no more than 3 pages and the Financial Plan *(primarily Capital Requirements and Use of Proceeds).* When you are writing the Executive Summary, remember the Assessment Matrix in Chapter 1.

The difference between the Business Plan and the Marketing Plan is one is strategic and should be reviewed once a year and the other is largely tactical and should reviewed at least quarterly.

The Executive Summary
- Description of the business
- Uniqueness and positioning
- Capital requirements
- Management team
- The market
- Competition
- Risk/Opportunity
- Financial summary.

The Business
- Business description
- Products and service
- Management plan
- Operations plan
- Risk/Opportunity analysis.

Marketing Plan
- The market
- Market research
- Marketing strategy
- Pricing policy and sales terms
- Distribution and customer service
- Advertising and promotion
- Market forecast.

Financial Plan
- Capital requirements
- Use of proceeds
- Opening day balance sheet
- Start-up costs
- Break-even analysis
- Key financial ratios and formulae
- Pro forma balance sheet
- Pro forma income statements
- Pro forma cash flow statements
- Pro forma sales *(in units)*.

Appendix
- Resumes
- Product literature an brochures
- Major contracts and agreements
- Market research data
- Miscellaneous supporting material.

Marketing Plan Outline

I have put more detail in this section because this document should be updated frequently. On the Internet there are several sources to choose from. Your marketing plan can be in narrative form or in bullet form. It is for your use and to communicate to the other affected parties, so use the form you feel most comfortable with. You don't have to have a plan for each section, but it is important to consciously accept or reject the item. For example, you may not have a direct sales force, but still ask the question why and then proceed.

Market Summary
- Market: past, present, & future
    - Review changes in market share, leadership, market shifts, costs, pricing and competition.

Product Definition
- Describe product/service being marketed.

Competition
- The competitive landscape
    - Provide an overview of product competitors, their strengths and weaknesses
    - Position each competitor's product against new product or service.

Positioning
- Company positioning
- Positioning of product or service

- Customer promise
  - Statement summarizing the benefit of the product or service to the customer.

The 4 P's
- Product, Price, Place and Promotion.

Product
- The Product definition is the start of your promotional material including positioning, value and features/function benefits.

Price
- Pricing
  - Summarize specific pricing or pricing strategies
  - Compare to similar products.

Place/Channel Strategy
- Set by vertical, geographic territory, skill and customer access.

Channel Strategy
- Direct – territory/compensation
- Agent
- Distributor
- OEM
- Define overlap.

Vertical Markets/Segments
- Vertical market opportunities

- Specific market segment opportunities, distribution strategies and third-party partner roles in distribution to vertical markets.

Distribution
- Distribution strategy
- Channels of distribution.

International
- International distribution
- International pricing strategy
- Localization issues (e.g. labelling).

Product Packaging
Cost of goods and high-level bill of materials

Promotion
- Set your marketing objectives and measurements
- Promotional plan
- Relate back to positioning.

Success Metrics
- First year goals
- Additional year goals
- Measures of success/failure
- Requirements for success.

Launch Strategies
- Launch plan
- Promotion budget.

Communication Strategies
- Messaging by audience
- Target consumer demographics.

Public Relations
- Strategy & execution - don't forget the new media!

Advertising
- Strategy & execution.

Other Promotion
- Direct marketing
- Third-party marketing
- Marketing programs
  - Other promotional programs.

Schedule
- 18-month schedule highlights.

Budget

Integrated Marketing & Communications Checklist

- ✓ Is there clear positioning?
- ✓ Does the campaign have clear objectives and measurements?
- ✓ Do your objectives support your business plan?
- ✓ Are your strategies consistent with objectives and business values?
- ✓ Are all 4 "P's" in the plan and consistent with your objectives?
- ✓ Are the right marketing skills available?
- ✓ Do you have a pricing strategy?
- ✓ Is there something in each campaign aimed at all participants?
- ✓ Is what your website says about your company effective?
- ✓ Have you considered all audience segments?
- ✓ Is your plan targeted properly for each audience segment?
- ✓ Are your messages on strategy and positioning?
- ✓ Are you speaking the customer's language?
- ✓ Is your message relevant?
- ✓ Are your tactics consistent with the strategy? Will they get the desired results?
- ✓ Does your plan keep you in front of your audiences on an on-going basis?
- ✓ Is there a clear, consistent and explainable channel strategy?
- ✓ Do you have internal communication programs that support your strategies?
- ✓ Are the right feedback mechanisms in place? Do you have an audit plan for each activity?
- ✓ Can you make necessary adjustments in a cost-efficient manner?
- ✓ Does the plan fit your budget?
- ✓ Are you prepared to stay the course?

Product Launch Checklist

Take your new product or service and answer the questions below. Some of them may not apply but you need to consciously reject them, rather than overlook something:

Customer Questions
- Who is the end customer?
- How many are there?
- Where are they?
- What are the key buying criteria?

Product Questions
- What is the unique selling proposition of the product?
- Who is the competition?
    - What are their strengths/weaknesses?
    - What are they likely to do?
- What is the pricing strategy?

Channel
- Who are the channels?
- What are their key buying criteria?
- Do they know the customers?
- Do they stock, consign or order for customer fulfillment?
- What are their strengths/weaknesses?
- Are they trained?

Sales Force
- Who are their contacts and are they related to the end customers and channels for this product?
- What are their skills related to the product?

- Are they trained?
- Are their incentives sufficient?

Stakeholders
- Are they informed of the product, company and direction?
- Are they adequately trained?
- Are they supportive?

Overall
- What are the measurements and objectives?
    - What are your objectives for the first 3 months?
- Sales, awareness, market penetration, web hits, inquiries?
    - What are your objectives for the next 9 months?
- Sales, competitive position, etc.?

Financial Management Checklist

- ✓ Is there a clear, concise summary of results available?
- ✓ Are the reports produced on a timely basis?
- ✓ Are the reports understandable, not overwhelmed by detail?
- ✓ Can the system/model accommodate new departments?
- ✓ Are there any complaints from various stakeholders?
- ✓ Are department heads held accountable for their results?
- ✓ Are peak financing requirements known?
- ✓ Are there good explanations of variances?
- ✓ Do accounting/finance people have necessary skills?
- ✓ Are there significant year-end adjustments by auditors? *(This is often a sign of trouble in your systems.)*
- ✓ Do the financial people communicate with operations, sales, etc.?

Funding Checklist

- ✓ Do you have a business plan?
- ✓ Do you have a marketing plan?
- ✓ Do you know what the funds will be used for?
- ✓ Do you know how much money you need and when?
- ✓ Do you know the minimum amount required for survival?
- ✓ Have you considered all possible sources?
- ✓ Are you currently tapping into what you control?

Human Resources Checklist

- ✓ Does your business strategy address human resources?
- ✓ Have you capitalized on some of the key demographic trends?
- ✓ Do you hire based on competency profiles or "gut" opinion?
- ✓ Can you accurately describe your culture to potential hires?
- ✓ Have you developed an employee retention strategy?
- ✓ Do you conduct organizational effectiveness scans?
- ✓ Have you contemplated areas for outsourcing?

GLOSSARY

Bleeding Edge Technology – Leading edge technology is new and innovative. Bleeding edge technology is so new it carries high risk. In early aviation, the Wright Brothers plane was bleeding edge; the Red Baron's tri-plane was leading edge.

VC – Venture Capitalist.

Floor Financing – a type of asset-based financing, is a method of financing the of a business. Terms of repayment are matched to the nature of the business with special provisions for rental inventory and seasonal adjustments consistent with the sales cycle. Many large banks and specialty financing firms (e.g., GE Capital) offer floor financing.

Usury – Obscenely high interest rates.

ABOUT THE AUTHOR

David Morrison is a retired Information Technology Executive with over three decades of industry experience. Most recently as the President of Cognoscente Consulting Ltd., David worked around the globe leveraging his keen understanding of product technology and his strong operations background to help a number of start-up and small businesses get off the ground. By applying his knowledge of product and business development, along with his marketing and management expertise, David has helped many companies achieve measurable success through re-engineering and restructuring their processes.

During his tenure at IBM, David was responsible for developing and managing many of the new initiatives instituted by the Company in launching and operating their PC business. This included setting up a wholly autonomous division to produce the Ambra clones and the restructuring of the IBM Consumer Products Division. In addition to working with MicroSoft and Intel, David took a lead role in creating one of the first ever customer call centers. After leaving IBM, he was Chief Operating Executive of a startup manufacturer called IPS Automation later purchased by Photon

Dynamics. He then served as President of Highway Software, a Dotcom era software company.

Throughout his career David consulted to several large and medium businesses on marketing issues, and process engineering and finished his working career managing a division of Applanix Corporation, another small technology company. David has served on the board of directors for several companies. David currently assists third world businesses through the Canadian Executive Service Organization (CESO) and also volunteers through Rotary in Canada and in Panama. He has a BASc in Electrical Engineering, a MASc in Process Control Systems, an MBA and is a graduate of IBM's Systems Research Institute.

Author David Morrison

Visit My Blog: http://roadrunnerorroadkill.typepad.com/

Made in the USA
Charleston, SC
01 June 2010